PHRASEBOOK

— MALAY —

By Andrey Taranov

THE MOST IMPORTANT PHRASES

This phrasebook contains
the most important
phrases and questions
for basic communication
Everything you need
to survive overseas

T&P BOOKS

Phrasebook + 3000-word dictionary

English-Malay phrasebook & topical vocabulary

By Andrey Taranov

The collection of "Everything Will Be Okay" travel phrasebooks published by T&P Books is designed for people traveling abroad for tourism and business. The phrasebooks contain what matters most - the essentials for basic communication. This is an indispensable set of phrases to "survive" while abroad.

This book also includes a small topical vocabulary that contains roughly 3,000 of the most frequently used words. Another section of the phrasebook provides a gastronomical dictionary that may help you order food at a restaurant or buy groceries at the store.

T&P Books Publishing
www.tpbooks.com

ISBN: 978-1-83955-082-9

This book is also available in E-book formats.
Please visit www.tpbooks.com or the major online bookstores.

FOREWORD

The collection of "Everything Will Be Okay" travel phrasebooks published by T&P Books is designed for people traveling abroad for tourism and business. The phrasebooks contain what matters most - the essentials for basic communication. This is an indispensable set of phrases to "survive" while abroad.

This phrasebook will help you in most cases where you need to ask something, get directions, find out how much something costs, etc. It can also resolve difficult communication situations where gestures just won't help.

This book contains a lot of phrases that have been grouped according to the most relevant topics. The edition also includes a small vocabulary that contains roughly 3,000 of the most frequently used words. Another section of the phrasebook provides a gastronomical dictionary that may help you order food at a restaurant or buy groceries at the store.

Take "Everything Will Be Okay" phrasebook with you on the road and you'll have an irreplaceable traveling companion who will help you find your way out of any situation and teach you to not fear speaking with foreigners.

TABLE OF CONTENTS

T&P Books Publishing

PRONUNCIATION

T&P phonetic alphabet	Malay example	English example

Vowels

[a]	naskhah [naskah]	shorter than in ask
[e]	lebar [lebar]	elm, medal
[ɛ]	teman [tɛman]	man, bad
[i]	lidah [lidah]	shorter than in feet
[o]	blok [blok]	pod, John
[u]	kebun [kɛbun]	book

Consonants

[b]	burung [buruŋ]	baby, book
[d]	dunia [dunia]	day, doctor
[dʒ]	panjang [pandʒaŋ]	joke, general
[f]	platform [platform]	face, food
[g]	granit [granit]	game, gold
[ɣ]	spaghetti [spaɣeti]	between [g] and [h]
[j]	layar [lajar]	yes, New York
[h]	matahari [matahari]	home, have
[k]	mekanik [mekanik]	clock, kiss
[l]	lelaki [lɛlaki]	lace, people
[m]	memukul [mɛmukul]	magic, milk
[n]	nenek [nenek]	name, normal
[ŋ]	gunung [gunuŋ]	English, ring
[p]	pemuda [pɛmuda]	pencil, private
[r]	rakyat [rakjat]	rice, radio
[s]	sembuh [sɛmbuh]	city, boss
[ʃ]	champagne [ʃampejn]	machine, shark
[t]	matematik [matɛmatik]	tourist, trip
[x]	akhirat [axirat]	as in Scots 'loch'
[tʃ]	cacing [tʃatʃiŋ]	church, French
[ɕ]	syurga [ɕurga]	sheep, shop
[v]	Taiwan [tajvan]	very, river
[z]	zuriat [zuriat]	zebra, please
[w]	penguasa [pɛŋwasa]	vase, winter

LIST OF ABBREVIATIONS

English abbreviations

ab.	-	about
adj	-	adjective
adv	-	adverb
anim.	-	animate
as adj	-	attributive noun used as adjective
e.g.	-	for example
etc.	-	et cetera
fam.	-	familiar
fem.	-	feminine
form.	-	formal
inanim.	-	inanimate
masc.	-	masculine
math	-	mathematics
mil.	-	military
n	-	noun
pl	-	plural
pron.	-	pronoun
sb	-	somebody
sing.	-	singular
sth	-	something
v aux	-	auxiliary verb
vi	-	intransitive verb
vi, vt	-	intransitive, transitive verb
vt	-	transitive verb

MALAY PHRASEBOOK

This section contains
important phrases that may
come in handy in various
real-life situations.
The phrasebook will help
you ask for directions, clarify
a price, buy tickets, and
order food at a restaurant

T&P Books Publishing

PHRASEBOOK
CONTENTS

T&P Books Publishing

The bare minimum

Excuse me, ...	**Maaf, ...** [Maaf, ...]
Hello.	**Salam sejahtera.** [Salam sedʒahtera.]
Thank you.	**Terima kasih.** [Terimə kasih.]
Good bye.	**Sampai jumpa lagi.** [Sampai dʒumpə lagi.]
Yes.	**Ya.** [Ya.]
No.	**Tidak.** [Tida.]
I don't know.	**Saya tidak tahu.** [Sayə tida tahu.]
Where? | Where to? | When?	**Di mana? | Ke mana? | Bila?** [Di mana? | Ke mana? | Bila?]
I need ...	**Saya perlukan ...** [Sayə perlukan ...]
I want ...	**Saya mahu ...** [Sayə mahu ...]
Do you have ...?	**Anda ada ...?** [Andə ada ...?]
Is there a ... here?	**Di sini ada ...?** [Di sini ada ...?]
May I ...?	**Boleh saya ...?** [Boleh saya ...?]
..., please (polite request)	**Silahkan** [Silahkan]
I'm looking for ...	**Saya cari ...** [Sayə tʃari ...]
the restroom	**tandas** [tandas]
an ATM	**ATM** [ateem]
a pharmacy (drugstore)	**kedai ubat** [kedai ubat]
a hospital	**hospital** [hospital]
the police station	**balai polis** [balai polis]
the subway	**LRT** [elerte]

a taxi	**teksi** [teksi]
the train station	**stesen kereta api** [stesen kereta api]

My name is …	**Nama saya …** [Namə saya …]
What's your name?	**Siapa nama anda?** [Siapə namə anda?]
Could you please help me?	**Silahkan tolong saya.** [Silahkan toloŋ saya.]
I've got a problem.	**Saya ada masalah.** [Sayə adə masalah.]
I don't feel well.	**Saya kurang enak badan.** [Sayə kuraŋ ena badan.]
Call an ambulance!	**Tolong panggil ambulans!** [Toloŋ paŋgil ambulans!]
May I make a call?	**Boleh saya telefon?** [Boleh sayə telefon?]

I'm sorry.	**Maaf** [Maaf]
You're welcome.	**Sama-sama** [Sama-samə]

I, me	**saya** [sayə]
you (inform.)	**awak** [awa]
he	**dia** [diə]
she	**dia** [diə]
they (masc.)	**mereka** [merekə]
they (fem.)	**mereka** [merekə]
we	**kita, kami** [kita, kami]
you (pl)	**kamu sekalian** [kamu sekalian]
you (sg, form.)	**Anda** [Andə]

ENTRANCE	**MASUK** [masu]
EXIT	**keluar** [keluar]
OUT OF ORDER	**rosak** [rosa]
CLOSED	**tutup** [tutup]

OPEN

BUKA
[bukə]

FOR WOMEN

untuk perempuan
[untu perempuan]

FOR MEN

untuk lelaki
[untu lelaki]

Questions

Where?	**Di mana?** [Di mana?]
Where to?	**Ke mana?** [Ke mana?]
Where from?	**Dari mana?** [Dari mana?]
Why?	**Mengapa?** [Meŋapa?]
For what reason?	**Fasal apa?** [Fasal apa?]
When?	**Bila?** [Bila?]
How long?	**Berapa lama?** [Berapə lama?]
At what time?	**Pukul berapa?** [Pukul berapa?]
How much?	**Berapa harga?** [Berapə harga?]
Do you have ...?	**Anda ada ...?** [Andə ada ...?]
Where is ...?	**Di mana terletak ...?** [Di manə terleta ...?]
What time is it?	**Pukul berapa?** [Pukul berapa?]
May I make a call?	**Boleh saya telefon?** [Boleh sayə telefon?]
Who's there?	**Siapa di situ?** [Siapə di situ?]
Can I smoke here?	**Boleh saya merokok di sini?** [Boleh sayə meroko di sini?]
May I ...?	**Boleh saya ...?** [Boleh saya ...?]

Needs

I'd like …	**Saya mahu …** [Sayə mahu …]
I don't want …	**Saya tidak mahu …** [Sayə tida mahu …]
I'm thirsty.	**Saya mahu minum.** [Sayə mahu minum.]
I want to sleep.	**Saya mahu tidur.** [Sayə mahu tidur.]
I want …	**Saya mahu …** [Sayə mahu …]
to wash up	**membasuh muka** [membasuh mukə]
to brush my teeth	**menggosok gigi** [meŋgoso gigi]
to rest a while	**rehat sikit** [rehat sikit]
to change my clothes	**bersalin** [bersalin]
to go back to the hotel	**pulang ke hotel** [pulaŋ ke hotel]
to buy …	**beli …** [beli …]
to go to …	**pergi ke …** [pergi ke …]
to visit …	**melawat …** [melawat …]
to meet with …	**berjumpa dengan …** [berdʒumpə deŋan …]
to make a call	**telefon** [telefon]
I'm tired.	**Saya letih.** [Sayə letih.]
We are tired.	**Kami letih.** [Kami letih.]
I'm cold.	**Saya kesejukan.** [Sayə kesedʒukan.]
I'm hot.	**Saya kepanasan.** [Sayə kepanasan.]
I'm OK.	**Saya OK.** [Sayə okej.]

I need to make a call.   **Saya perlu telefon.**
[Saya perlu telefon.]

I need to go to the restroom.   **Saya perlu ke tandas.**
[Saya perlu ke tandas.]

I have to go.   **Saya perlu pulang.**
[Saya perlu pulaŋ.]

I have to go now.   **Saya perlu pergi.**
[Saya perlu pergi.]

Asking for directions

Excuse me, ...	**Maaf ...** [Maaf ...]
Where is ...?	**Di mana terletak ...?** [Di manə terleta ...?]
Which way is ...?	**Ke arah mana terletak ...?** [Ke arah manə terleta ...?]
Could you help me, please?	**Silahkan, tolong saya.** [Silahkan, toloŋ saya.]
I'm looking for ...	**Saya cari ...** [Sayə tʃari ...]
I'm looking for the exit.	**Saya cari pintu keluar.** [Sayə tʃari pintu keluar.]
I'm going to ...	**Saya pergi ke ...** [Sayə pergi ke ...]
Am I going the right way to ...?	**Saya pergi ke ... arah betul?** [Sayə pergi ke ... arah betul?]
Is it far?	**Ini jauhkah?** [Ini dʒauhkah?]
Can I get there on foot?	**Boleh saya sampai ke sana berjalan kaki?** [Boleh sayə sampai ke sanə berdʒalan kaki?]
Can you show me on the map?	**Silahkan, tunjukkan di peta.** [Silahkan, tundʒukkan di peta.]
Show me where we are right now.	**Tunjukkan di peta di mana kita sekarang.** [Tundʒukkan di petə di manə kitə sekaraŋ.]
Here	**Di sini** [Di sini]
There	**Di situ** [Di situ]
This way	**Jalan ini** [dʒalan ini]
Turn right.	**Belok ke kanan.** [Belo ke kanan.]
Turn left.	**Belok ke kiri.** [Belo ke kiri.]
first (second, third) turn	**belokan pertama (kedua, ketiga)** [belokan pertamə (kedua, ketiga)]

to the right

ke kanan
[ke kanan]

to the left

ke kiri
[ke kiri]

Go straight ahead.

Pergi terus.
[Pergi terus.]

Signs

WELCOME! **SELAMAT DATANG!**
[selamat dataŋ!]

ENTRANCE **MASUK**
[masu]

EXIT **KELUAR**
[keluar]

PUSH **TOLAK**
[tola]

PULL **TARIK**
[tari]

OPEN **BUKA**
[bukə]

CLOSED **TUTUP**
[tutup]

FOR WOMEN **UNTUK PEREMPUAN**
[untu perempuan]

FOR MEN **UNTUK LELAKI**
[untu lelaki]

GENTLEMEN, GENTS **TANDAS LELAKI**
[tandas lelaki]

WOMEN **TANDAS PEREMPUAN**
[tandas perempuan]

DISCOUNTS **POTONGAN**
[potoŋan]

SALE **JUALAN MURAH**
[dʒualan murah]

FREE **PERCUMA**
[pertʃumə]

NEW! **BARANG BARU!**
[baraŋ baru!]

ATTENTION! **PERHATIAN!**
[perhatian!]

NO VACANCIES **TIDAK ADA TEMPAT KOSONG**
[tida adə tempat kosoŋ]

RESERVED **DITEMPAH**
[ditempah]

ADMINISTRATION **PENTADBIRAN**
[pentadbiran]

STAFF ONLY **UNTUK KAKITANGAN SAJA**
[untu kakitaŋan sadʒə]

BEWARE OF THE DOG!	**ANJING GANAS** [andʒiŋ ganas]
NO SMOKING!	**DILARANG MEROKOK!** [dilaraŋ merokok!]
DO NOT TOUCH!	**JANGAN SENTUH!** [dʒaŋan sentuh!]
DANGEROUS	**BERBAHAYA** [berbahayə]
DANGER	**BAHAYA** [bahayə]
HIGH VOLTAGE	**VOLTAN TINGGI** [voltan tiŋgi]
NO SWIMMING!	**DILARANG BERENANG** [dilaraŋ berenaŋ]
OUT OF ORDER	**ROSAK** [rosa]
FLAMMABLE	**MUDAH TERBAKAR** [mudah terbakar]
FORBIDDEN	**DILARANG** [dilaraŋ]
NO TRESPASSING!	**TIDAK ADA LALUAN TERUS** [tida adə laluan terus]
WET PAINT	**CAT BASAH** [tʃat basah]
CLOSED FOR RENOVATIONS	**TUTUP UNTUK DIPERBAIKI** [tutup untu diperbaiki]
WORKS AHEAD	**KERJA GALIAN** [kerdʒə galian]
DETOUR	**LENCONGAN** [lentʃoŋan]

Transportation. General phrases

plane	**kapal terbang** [kapal terbaŋ]
train	**kereta api, tren** [keretə api, tren]
bus	**bas** [bas]
ferry	**feri** [feri]
taxi	**teksi** [teksi]
car	**kereta** [keretə]
schedule	**jadual** [dʒadual]
Where can I see the schedule?	**Di mana saya boleh melihat jadual?** [Di manə sayə boleh melihat dʒadual?]
workdays (weekdays)	**hari-hari kerja** [hari-hari kerdʒə]
weekends	**hari-hari cuti** [hari-hari ʧuti]
holidays	**hari-hari perayaan** [hari-hari perayaan]
DEPARTURE	**PERLEPASAN** [perlepasan]
ARRIVAL	**KETIBAAN** [ketibaan]
DELAYED	**TERLAMBAT** [terlambat]
CANCELLED	**DIBATALKAN** [dibatalkan]
next (train, etc.)	**seterusnya (tren dll)** [seterusnyə]
first	**pertama** [pertamə]
last	**terakhir** [teraχir]
When is the next ...?	**Bila ... seterusnya akan tiba?** [Bilə ... seterusnyə akan tiba?]
When is the first ...?	**Bila ... seterusnya akan berlepas?** [Bilə ... seterusnyə akan berlepas?]

When is the last ...?

Bila ... terakhir akan berlepas
[Bilə ... teraχir akan berlepas]

transfer (change of trains, etc.)

pertukaran
[pertukaran]

to make a transfer

membuat pertukaran
[membuat pertukaran]

Do I need to make a transfer?

Perlukah saya membuat pertukaran?
[Perlukah sayə membuat pertukaran?]

Buying tickets

Where can I buy tickets?	**Di mana saya boleh membeli tiket?** [Di manə sayə boleh membeli tiket?]
to buy a ticket	**membeli tiket** [membeli tiket]
ticket price	**harga tiket** [hargə tiket]
Where to?	**Ke mana?** [Ke manə?]
To what station?	**Sampai stesen yang mana?** [Sampai stesen yaŋ manə?]
I need ...	**Saya perlukan ...** [Sayə perlukan ...]
one ticket	**satu tiket** [satu tiket]
two tickets	**dua tiket** [duə tiket]
three tickets	**tiga tiket** [tigə tiket]
one-way	**perjalanan sehala** [perdʒalanan sehalə]
round-trip	**pergi balik** [pergi bali]
first class	**kelas satu** [kelas satu]
second class	**kelas dua** [kelas duə]
today	**hari ini** [hari ini]
tomorrow	**besok** [beso]
the day after tomorrow	**besok lusa** [beso lusə]
in the morning	**pagi** [pagi]
in the afternoon	**siang hari** [siaŋ hari]
in the evening	**petang** [petaŋ]

aisle seat

tempat pada laluan
[tempat padə laluan]

window seat

tempat pada tingkap
[tempat padə tiŋkap]

How much?

Berapa?
[Berapa?]

Can I pay by credit card?

Boleh saya bayar dengan kad?
[Boleh sayə bayar deŋan kad?]

Bus

bus	**bas** [bas]
intercity bus	**bas anara bandar** [bas anarə bandar]
bus stop	**perhentian bas** [perhentian bas]
Where's the nearest bus stop?	**Di mana perhentian bas yang terdekat?** [Di manə perhentian bas yaŋ terdekat?]
number (bus ~, etc.)	**nombor** [nombor]
Which bus do I take to get to …?	**Bas nombor berapa pergi sampai …?** [Bas nombor berapə pergi sampai …?]
Does this bus go to …?	**Adakah bas ini pergi sampai …?** [Adakah bas ini pergi sampai …?]
How frequent are the buses?	**Berapa kerap bas ini pergi?** [Berapə kerap bas ini pergi?]
every 15 minutes	**setiap 15 minit** [setiap lima belas minit]
every half hour	**setiap setengah jam** [setiap seteŋah dʒam]
every hour	**setiap jam** [setiap dʒam]
several times a day	**beberapa kali sehari** [beberapə kali sehari]
… times a day	**… kali sehari** [… kali sehari]
schedule	**jadual** [dʒadual]
Where can I see the schedule?	**Di mana saya boleh melihat jadual?** [Di manə sayə boleh melihat dʒadual?]
When is the next bus?	**Bila bas seterusnya tiba?** [Bilə bas seterusnyə tiba?]
When is the first bus?	**Bila bas pertama berlepas?** [Bilə bas pertamə berlepas?]
When is the last bus?	**Bila bas terakhir berlepas?** [Bilə bas teraχir berlepas?]

stop

perhentian
[perhentian]

next stop

perhentian seterusnya
[perhentian seterusnyə]

last stop (terminus)

perhentian terakhir
[perhentian teraχir]

Stop here, please.

Tolong berhenti di sini.
[Toloŋ berhenti di sini.]

Excuse me, this is my stop.

Maaf, ini perhentian saya.
[Maaf, ini perhentian saya.]

Train

train	**kereta api, tren** [keretə api, tren]
suburban train	**komuter** [komuter]
long-distance train	**kereta api jarak jauh** [keretə api dʒara dʒauh]
train station	**stesen kereta api** [stesen keretə api]
Excuse me, where is the exit to the platform?	**Maaf, di mana laluan ke kereta api?** [Maaf, di manə laluan kə keretə api?]
Does this train go to ...?	**Adakah kereta api ini pergi ke ...?** [Adakah keretə api ini pergi ke ...?]
next train	**kereta api seterusnya** [keretə api seterusnyə]
When is the next train?	**Bila kereta api seterusnya berlepas?** [Bilə keretə api seterusnyə berlepas?]
Where can I see the schedule?	**Di mana saya boleh melihat jadual?** [Di manə sayə boleh melihat dʒadual?]
From which platform?	**Dari platform nombor berapa?** [Dari platform nombor berapa?]
When does the train arrive in ...?	**Bila kereta api sampai ke ...?** [Bilə keretə api sampai ke ...?]
Please help me.	**Silahkan, tolong saya.** [Silahkan, toloŋ saya.]
I'm looking for my seat.	**Saya cari tempat saya.** [Sayə tʃari tempat saya.]
We're looking for our seats.	**Kami cari tempat kami.** [Kami tʃari tempat kami.]
My seat is taken.	**Tempat saya dipakai.** [Tempat sayə dipakai.]
Our seats are taken.	**Tempat kami dipakai.** [Tempat kami dipakai.]
I'm sorry but this is my seat.	**Maaf, tetapi tempat ini saya punya.** [Maaf, tetapi tempat ini sayə punya.]
Is this seat taken?	**Tempat ini kosong?** [Tempat ini kosoŋ?]
May I sit here?	**Boleh saya duduk di sini?** [Boleh sayə dudu di sini?]

On the train. Dialogue (No ticket)

Ticket, please.

Silahkan, pamerkan tiket anda.
[Silahkan, pamerkan tiket anda.]

I don't have a ticket.

Saya tidak ada tiket.
[Saya tida ada tiket.]

I lost my ticket.

Saya kehilangan tiket.
[Saya kehilaŋan tiket.]

I forgot my ticket at home.

Saya tertinggal tiket di rumah.
[Saya tertiŋgal tiket di rumah.]

You can buy a ticket from me.

Anda boleh membeli tiket pada saya.
[Anda boleh membeli tiket pada saya.]

You will also have to pay a fine.

Anda terpaksa juga membayar denda.
[Anda terpaksa dʒuga membayar denda.]

Okay.

Baiklah.
[Baiklah.]

Where are you going?

Anda pergi ke mana?
[Anda pergi ke mana?]

I'm going to …

Saya pergi ke …
[Saya pergi ke …]

How much? I don't understand.

Berapa? Saya tidak faham.
[Berapa? Saya tida faham.]

Write it down, please.

Silahkan, tulis.
[Silahkan, tulis.]

Okay. Can I pay with a credit card?

Baik. Boleh saya bayar dengan kad?
[Bai. Boleh saya bayar deŋan kad?]

Yes, you can.

Ya, boleh.
[Ya, boleh.]

Here's your receipt.

Ini resit anda.
[Ini resit anda.]

Sorry about the fine.

Maaf kerana anda kena denda.
[Maaf kerana anda kena denda.]

That's okay. It was my fault.

Tidak apa-apa. Itu salah saya.
[Tida apa-apa. Itu salah saya.]

Enjoy your trip.

Selamat jalan.
[Selamat dʒalan.]

Taxi

taxi	**teksi** [teksi]
taxi driver	**pemandu teksi** [pemandu teksi]
to catch a taxi	**menangkap teksi** [menaŋkap teksi]
taxi stand	**perhentian teksi** [perhentian teksi]
Where can I get a taxi?	**Di mana saya boleh menyewa teksi?** [Di manə sayə boleh menyewə teksi?]
to call a taxi	**memanggil teksi** [memaŋgil teksi]
I need a taxi.	**Saya perlukan teksi.** [Sayə perlukan teksi.]
Right now.	**Sekarang juga.** [Sekaraŋ dʒuga.]
What is your address (location)?	**Alamat anda?** [Alamat anda?]
My address is ...	**Alamat saya ...** [Alamat saya ...]
Your destination?	**Anda pergi ke mana?** [Andə pergi ke mana?]
Excuse me, ...	**Maaf, ...** [Maaf, ...]
Are you available?	**Teksi ini kosong?** [Teksi ini kosoŋ?]
How much is it to get to ...?	**Berapa tambang sampai ...?** [Berapə tambaŋ sampai ...?]
Do you know where it is?	**Anda tahu, di mana itu?** [Andə tahu, di manə itu?]
Airport, please.	**Silahkan, ke lapangan terbang.** [Silahkan, ke lapaŋan terbaŋ.]
Stop here, please.	**Silahkan berhenti di sini.** [Silahkan berhenti di sini.]
It's not here.	**Bukan di sini.** [Bukan di sini.]
This is the wrong address.	**Alamat itu salah.** [Alamat itu salah.]
Turn left.	**Sekarang ke kiri.** [Sekaraŋ ke kiri.]
Turn right.	**Sekarang ke kanan.** [Sekaraŋ ke kanan.]

How much do I owe you?

Berapa saya harus bayar?
[Berapǝ sayǝ harus bayar?]

I'd like a receipt, please.

Silahkan, bagi resit.
[Silahkan, bagi resit.]

Keep the change.

Simpan baki.
[Simpan baki.]

Would you please wait for me?

Silahkan tunggu saya di sini.
[Silahkan tuŋgu sayǝ di sini.]

five minutes

lima minit
[limǝ minit]

ten minutes

sepuluh minit
[sepuluh minit]

fifteen minutes

lima belas minit
[limǝ belas minit]

twenty minutes

dua puluh minit
[duǝ puluh minit]

half an hour

setengah jam
[seteŋah dʒam]

Hotel

Hello.	**Salam sejahtera.** [Salam sedʒahtera.]
My name is …	**Nama saya …** [Namə saya …]
I have a reservation.	**Saya menempah bilik.** [Sayə menempah bili.]
I need …	**Saya perlukan …** [Sayə perlukan …]
a single room	**bilik untuk satu orang** [bili untu satu oraŋ]
a double room	**bilik untuk dua orang** [bili untu duə oraŋ]
How much is that?	**Berapa harganya?** [Berapə harganya?]
That's a bit expensive.	**Itu mahal sikit.** [Itu mahal sikit.]
Do you have anything else?	**Anda ada bilik lain?** [Andə adə bili lain?]
I'll take it.	**Saya akan menerimanya.** [Sayə akan menerimanya.]
I'll pay in cash.	**Saya akan bayar wang tunai.** [Sayə akan bayar waŋ tunai.]
I've got a problem.	**Saya ada masalah.** [Sayə adə masalah.]
My … is broken.	**… saya rosak.** [… sayə rosa.]
My … is out of order.	**… saya tidak berfungsi.** [… sayə tida berfuŋsi.]
TV	**peti televisyen** [peti televiçen]
air conditioner	**penghawa dingin** [penɣawə diŋin]
tap	**pili** [pili]
shower	**pancutan air** [pantʃutan air]
sink	**sink cuci tangan** [sin tʃutʃi taŋan]
safe	**peti besi** [peti besi]

door lock	**kunci pintu** [kuntʃi pintu]
electrical outlet	**soket** [soket]
hairdryer	**kipas angin** [kipas aŋin]

I don't have …	**Saya tidak ada …** [Saya tida ada …]
water	**air** [air]
light	**api** [api]
electricity	**elektrik** [elektri]

Can you give me …?	**Boleh anda beri …?** [Boleh anda beri …?]
a towel	**tuala** [tuala]
a blanket	**selimut** [selimut]
slippers	**selipar** [selipar]
a robe	**jubah** [dʒubah]
shampoo	**syampu** [ɕampu]
soap	**sabun** [sabun]

I'd like to change rooms.	**Saya nak tukar bilik.** [Saya na tukar bili.]
I can't find my key.	**Saya tak boleh menemui kunci saya.** [Saya ta boleh menemui kuntʃi saya.]
Could you open my room, please?	**Silahkan buka bilik saya.** [Silahkan buka bili saya.]
Who's there?	**Siapa di situ?** [Siapa di situ?]
Come in!	**Masuk!** [Masuk!]
Just a minute!	**Sekejap!** [Sekedʒap!]
Not right now, please.	**Silahkan, bukan sekarang.** [Silahkan, bukan sekaraŋ.]

Come to my room, please.	**Silahkan, masuk bilik saya.** [Silahkan, masu bili saya.]
I'd like to order food service.	**Saya mahu menempah makanan ke bilik.** [Saya mahu menempah makanan ke bili.]

My room number is …	**Nombor bilik saya …** [Nombor bili saya …]
I'm leaving …	**Saya mahu pergi …** [Saye mahu pergi …]
We're leaving …	**Kami mahu pergi …** [Kami mahu pergi …]
right now	**sekarang** [sekaraŋ]
this afternoon	**hari ini selepas tengah hari** [hari ini selepas teŋah hari]
tonight	**hari ini petang** [hari ini petaŋ]
tomorrow	**besok** [beso]
tomorrow morning	**besok pagi** [beso pagi]
tomorrow evening	**besok petang** [beso petaŋ]
the day after tomorrow	**besok lusa** [beso luse]

I'd like to pay.	**Saya nak membayar.** [Saye na membayar.]
Everything was wonderful.	**Segalanya baik sekali.** [Segalanye bai sekali.]
Where can I get a taxi?	**Di mana saya boleh mengambil teksi?** [Di mane saye boleh meŋambil teksi?]
Would you call a taxi for me, please?	**Silahkan panggil teksi.** [Silahkan paŋgil teksi.]

Restaurant

Can I look at the menu, please?
Boleh saya tengok menu?
[Boleh saya teŋo menu?]

Table for one.
Meja untuk satu orang.
[Medʒə untu satu oraŋ.]

There are two (three, four) of us.
Kami dua (tiga, empat) orang.
[Kami duə (tiga, empat) oraŋ.]

Smoking
untuk perokok
[untu peroko]

No smoking
untuk bukan perokok
[untu bukan peroko]

Excuse me! (addressing a waiter)
Maaf!
[Maaf!]

menu
menu
[menu]

wine list
daftar wain
[daftar wain]

The menu, please.
Tolong bagi menu.
[Toloŋ bagi menu.]

Are you ready to order?
Anda sudah sedia menempah?
[Andə sudah sediə menempah?]

What will you have?
Apa yang anda mahu tempah?
[Apə yaŋ andə mahu tempah?]

I'll have …
Saya mahu …
[Sayə mahu …]

I'm a vegetarian.
Saya vegetarian.
[Sayə vegetarian.]

meat
daging
[dagiŋ]

fish
ikan
[ikan]

vegetables
sayur-sayuran
[sayur-sayuran]

Do you have vegetarian dishes?
Adakah di sini makanan vegetarian?
[Adakah di sini makanan vegetarian?]

I don't eat pork.
Saya tidak makan daging babi.
[Sayə tida makan dagiŋ babi.]

He /she/ doesn't eat meat.
Dia tidak makan daging.
[Diə tida makan dagiŋ.]

I am allergic to …
Saya alah terhadap …
[Sayə alah terhadap …]

Would you please bring me ...

Tolong bawa ...
[Toloŋ bawa ...]

salt | pepper | sugar

garam | lada | gula
[garam | lada | gulə]

coffee | tea | dessert

kopi | teh | cuci mulut
[kopi | teh | tʃutʃi mulut]

water | sparkling | plain

air | bergas | tidak bergas
[air | bergas | tida bergas]

a spoon | fork | knife

sudu | garpu | pisau
[sudu | garpu | pisau]

a plate | napkin

pinggan | tisu
[piŋgan | tisu]

Enjoy your meal!

Selamat jamu selera!
[Selamat dʒamu selera!]

One more, please.

Silahkan bawa lagi.
[Silahkan bawə lagi.]

It was very delicious.

Itu sedap sekali.
[Itu sedap sekali.]

---

check | change | tip

bil | wang baki | duit kopi
[bil | waŋ baki | duit kopi]

Check, please.
(Could I have the check, please?)

Tolong bawa bil.
[Toloŋ bawə bil.]

Can I pay by credit card?

Boleh saya bayar dengan kad?
[Boleh sayə bayar deŋan kad?]

I'm sorry, there's a mistake here.

Maaf, ada salah hitung.
[Maaf, adə salah hituŋ.]

Shopping

Can I help you?	**Boleh saya tolong kepada anda?** [Boleh saya toloŋ kepadə anda?]
Do you have ...?	**Di sini ada ...?** [Di sini ada ...?]
I'm looking for ...	**Saya cari ...** [Sayə ʧari ...]
I need ...	**Saya perlukan ...** [Sayə perlukan ...]
I'm just looking.	**Saya tengol-tengok saja.** [Sayə teŋol-teŋo sadʒa.]
We're just looking.	**Kami tengok-tengok saja.** [Kami teŋok-teŋo sadʒa.]
I'll come back later.	**Saya akan datang lebih kemudian.** [Sayə akan dataŋ lebih kemudian.]
We'll come back later.	**Kami akan datang lebih kemudian.** [Kami akan dataŋ lebih kemudian.]
discounts	sale	**potongan	jualan murah** [potoŋan	dʒualan murah]
Would you please show me ...	**Silahkan, pamerkan ...** [Silahkan, pamerkan ...]
Would you please give me ...	**Silahkan, bagi saya ...** [Silahkan, bagi saya ...]
Can I try it on?	**Boleh saya mencuba ini?** [Boleh sayə menʧubə ini?]
Excuse me, where's the fitting room?	**Maaf, dimana bilik acu?** [Maaf, dimanə bili aʧu?]
Which color would you like?	**Warna apa anda mahu?** [Warnə apə andə mahu?]
size	length	**ukuran	panjang** [ukuran	pandʒaŋ]
How does it fit?	**Sesuai?** [Sesuai?]
How much is it?	**Berapa harga ini?** [Berapə hargə ini?]
That's too expensive.	**Ini terlalu mahal.** [Ini terlalu mahal.]
I'll take it.	**Saya akan ambil ini.** [Sayə akan ambil ini.]
Excuse me, where do I pay?	**Maaf, di mana juruwang?** [Maaf, di manə dʒuruwaŋ?]

Will you pay in cash or credit card?

Bagaimana anda akan membayar?
Dengan wang tunai atau kad?
[Bagaimanə andə akan membayar?
Deŋan waŋ tunai atau kad?]

In cash | with credit card

dengan wang tunai | dengan kad
[deŋan waŋ tunai | deŋan kat]

Do you want the receipt?

Anda perlukan resit?
[Andə perlukan resit?]

Yes, please.

Ya, silahkan.
[Ya, silahkan.]

No, it's OK.

Tidak, tidak perlu. Terima kasih.
[Tida, tida perlu. Terimə kasih.]

Thank you. Have a nice day!

Terima kasih. Jumpa lagi!
[Terimə kasih. dʒumpə lagi!]

In town

Excuse me, ...	**Silahkan, maaf ...** [Silahkan, maaf ...]
I'm looking for ...	**Saya cari ...** [Sayə ʧari ...]
the subway	**LRT** [elerte]
my hotel	**hotel saya** [hotel sayə]
the movie theater	**pawagam** [pawagam]
a taxi stand	**perhentian teksi** [perhentian teksi]
an ATM	**ATM** [ateem]
a foreign exchange office	**pengurut wang** [peŋurut waŋ]
an internet café	**kafe siber** [kafe siber]
... street	**jalan ...** [dʒalan ...]
this place	**tempat ini** [tempat ini]
Do you know where ... is?	**Anda tahu di mana terletak ...?** [Andə tahu di manə terleta ...?]
Which street is this?	**Apa nama jalan ini?** [Apə namə dʒalan ini?]
Show me where we are right now.	**Tunjukkan di peta, di mana kita berada sekarang.** [Tundʒukkan di peta, di manə kitə beradə sekaraŋ.]
Can I get there on foot?	**Bolehkah saya sampai ke situ berjalan kaki?** [Bolehkah sayə sampai ke situ berdʒalan kaki?]
Do you have a map of the city?	**Anda ada peta bandar?** [Andə adə petə bandar?]
How much is a ticket to get in?	**Berapa harga tiket masuk?** [Berapə hargə tiket masuk?]
Can I take pictures here?	**Bolehkah di sini buat foto?** [Bolehkah di sini buat foto?]
Are you open?	**Ini buka?** [Ini buka?]

When do you open?

Pukul berapa ini buka?
[Pukul berapə ini buka?]

When do you close?

Sampai pukul berapa ini buka?
[Sampai pukul berapə ini buka?]

Money

money	**wang** [waŋ]
cash	**wang tunai** [waŋ tunai]
paper money	**wang kertas** [waŋ kertas]
loose change	**wang syiling** [waŋ çiliŋ]
check | change | tip	**bil | wang sisa | duit kopi** [bil | waŋ sisa | duit kopi]
credit card	**kad kredit** [kat kredit]
wallet	**dompet** [dompet]
to buy	**membeli** [membeli]
to pay	**membayar** [membayar]
fine	**denda** [dendə]
free	**percuma** [pertʃumə]
Where can I buy ...?	**Di mana saya boleh beli ...?** [Di manə sayə boleh beli ...?]
Is the bank open now?	**Bank ini sekarang buka?** [Ban ini sekaraŋ buka?]
When does it open?	**Pukul berapa ia buka?** [Pukul berapə iə buka?]
When does it close?	**Sampai pukul berapa ia buka?** [Sampai pukul berapə iə buka?]
How much?	**Berapa?** [Berapa?]
How much is this?	**Berapa harganya?** [Berapə harganya?]
That's too expensive.	**Ini terlalu mahal.** [Ini terlalu mahal.]
Excuse me, where do I pay?	**Maaf, di mana juruwang?** [Maaf, di manə dʒuruwaŋ?]
Check, please.	**Silahkan bawa bil.** [Silahkan bawə bil.]

Can I pay by credit card?	**Boleh saya bayar dengan kad?** [Boleh sayə bayar deŋan kad?]
Is there an ATM here?	**Ada di sini ATM?** [Adə di sini ateem?]
I'm looking for an ATM.	**Saya perlukan ATM.** [Sayə perlukan ateem.]

I'm looking for a foreign exchange office.	**Saya cari pengurut wang.** [Sayə tʃari peŋurut waŋ.]
I'd like to change …	**Saya nak tukar …** [Sayə na tukar …]
What is the exchange rate?	**Berapa kadar pertukaran?** [Berapə kadar pertukaran?]
Do you need my passport?	**Anda perlukan pasport saya?** [Andə perlukan pasport sayə?]

Time

What time is it?	**Pukul berapa?** [Pukul berapa?]
When?	**Bila?** [Bila?]
At what time?	**Pukul berapa?** [Pukul berapa?]
now | later | after …	**sekarang | kemudian | selepas …** [sekaraŋ | kemudian | selepas …]
one o'clock	**pukul satu tengah hari** [pukul satu teŋah hari]
one fifteen	**pukul satu suku** [pukul satu suku]
one thirty	**pukul satu setengah** [pukul satu seteŋah]
one forty-five	**pukul dua kurang suku** [pukul duə kuraŋ suku]
one | two | three	**satu | dua | tiga** [satu | dua | tigə]
four | five | six	**empat | lima | enam** [empat | lima | enam]
seven | eight | nine	**tujuh | lapan | sembilan** [tudʒuh | lapan | sembilan]
ten | eleven | twelve	**sepuluh | sebelas | dua belas** [sepuluh | sebelas | duə belas]
in …	**selepas …** [selepas …]
five minutes	**lima minit** [limə minit]
ten minutes	**sepuluh minit** [sepuluh minit]
fifteen minutes	**lima belas minit** [limə belas minit]
twenty minutes	**dua puluh minit** [duə puluh minit]
half an hour	**setengah jam** [seteŋah dʒam]
an hour	**satu jam** [satu dʒam]

in the morning	**pagi** [pagi]
early in the morning	**pagi-pagi** [pagi-pagi]
this morning	**pagi ini** [pagi ini]
tomorrow morning	**besok pagi** [beso pagi]
in the middle of the day	**tengah hari** [teŋah hari]
in the afternoon	**selepas tengah hari** [selepas teŋah hari]
in the evening	**petang** [petaŋ]
tonight	**petang ini** [petaŋ ini]
at night	**malam** [malam]
yesterday	**semalam** [semalam]
today	**hari ini** [hari ini]
tomorrow	**besok** [beso]
the day after tomorrow	**besok lusa** [beso lusə]
What day is it today?	**Hari ini hari apa?** [Hari ini hari apa?]
It's ...	**Hari ini ...** [Hari ini ...]
Monday	**Isnin** [Isnin]
Tuesday	**Selasa** [Selasə]
Wednesday	**Rabu** [Rabu]
Thursday	**Khamis** [χamis]
Friday	**Jumaat** [dʒumaat]
Saturday	**Sabtu** [Sabtu]
Sunday	**Ahad** [Ahat]

Greetings. Introductions

Hello.
Salam sejahtera.
[Salam sedʒahtera.]

Pleased to meet you.
Saya senang berkenalan dengan anda.
[Sayə senaŋ berkenalan deŋan anda.]

Me too.
Saya juga.
[Sayə dʒuga.]

I'd like you to meet …
Perkenalkan. Ini …
[Perkenalkan. Ini …]

Nice to meet you.
Salam berkenalan.
[Salam berkenalan.]

How are you?
Apa khabar?
[Apə χabar?]

My name is …
Nama saya …
[Namə saya …]

His name is …
Nama dia …
[Namə dia …]

Her name is …
Nama dia …
[Namə dia …]

What's your name?
Siapa nama anda?
[Siapə namə anda?]

What's his name?
Siapa namanya?
[Siapə namanya?]

What's her name?
Siapa namanya?
[Siapə namanya?]

What's your last name?
Siapa nama keluarga anda?
[Siapə namə keluargə anda?]

You can call me …
Panggil saya …
[Paŋgil saya …]

Where are you from?
Anda dari mana?
[Andə dari mana?]

I'm from …
Saya dari …
[Sayə dari …]

What do you do for a living?
Apa kerja anda?
[Apə kerdʒə anda?]

Who is this?
Siapa ini?
[Siapə ini?]

Who is he?
Siapa dia?
[Siapə dia?]

Who is she?	**Siapa dia?** [Siapə dia?]
Who are they?	**Siapa mereka?** [Siapə mereka?]

This is …	**Ini …** [Ini …]
my friend (masc.)	**sahabat saya** [sahabat sayə]
my friend (fem.)	**teman wanita saya** [teman wanitə sayə]
my husband	**suami saya** [suami sayə]
my wife	**isteri saya** [isteri sayə]

my father	**bapa saya** [bapə sayə]
my mother	**ibu saya** [ibu sayə]
my brother	**saudara saya** [saudarə sayə]
my sister	**sautara perempuan saya** [sautarə perempuan sayə]
my son	**anak lelaki saya** [ana lelaki sayə]
my daughter	**anak perempuan saya** [ana perempuan sayə]

This is our son.	**Ini anak lelaki kami.** [Ini ana lelaki kami.]
This is our daughter.	**Ini anak perempuan kami.** [Ini ana perempuan kami.]
These are my children.	**Ini anak-anak kami.** [Ini anak-ana kami.]

Farewells

Good bye!	**Sampai jumpa lagi!** [Sampai dʒumpə lagi!]
Bye! (inform.)	**Jumpa lagi!** [dʒumpə lagi!]
See you tomorrow.	**Sampai besok!** [Sampai besok!]
See you soon.	**Sampai bertemu lagi!** [Sampai bertemu lagi!]
See you at seven.	**Kita akan berjumpa pada pukul tujuh.** [Kitə akan berdʒumpə padə pukul tudʒuh.]
Have fun!	**Hiburkan diri!** [Hiburkan diri!]
Talk to you later.	**Kita akan bercakap kemudian.** [Kitə akan bertʃakap kemudian.]
Have a nice weekend.	**Selamat menikmati penghujung minggu ini.** [Selamat menikmati penɣudʒuŋ miŋgu ini.]
Good night.	**Selamat malam.** [Selamat malam.]
It's time for me to go.	**Masanya pulang.** [Masanyə pulaŋ.]
I have to go.	**Saya harus pulang.** [Sayə harus pulaŋ.]
I will be right back.	**Saya akan balik sekejap lagi.** [Sayə akan bali sekedʒap lagi.]
It's late.	**Sudah larut malam.** [Sudah larut malam.]
I have to get up early.	**Saya perlu bangun pagi-pagi.** [Sayə perlu baŋun pagi-pagi.]
I'm leaving tomorrow.	**Besok saya pulang.** [Beso sayə pulaŋ.]
We're leaving tomorrow.	**Besok kami pulang.** [Beso kami pulaŋ.]
Have a nice trip!	**Selamat jalan!** [Selamat dʒalan!]
It was nice meeting you.	**Senang berkenalan dengan anda.** [Senaŋ berkenalan deŋan anda.]

It was nice talking to you.	**Senang bergaul dengan anda.** [Senaŋ bergaul deŋan anda.]
Thanks for everything.	**Terima kasih atas segalanya.** [Terimə kasih atas segalanya.]

I had a very good time.	**Saya melepaskan masa dengan baik.** [Sayə melepaskan masə deŋan bai.]
We had a very good time.	**Kami melepaskan masa dengan baik.** [Kami melepaskan masə deŋan bai.]
It was really great.	**Segalanya bagus sekali.** [Segalanyə bagus sekali.]
I'm going to miss you.	**Saya akan rindu.** [Sayə akan rindu.]
We're going to miss you.	**Kami akan rindu.** [Kami akan rindu.]

Good luck!	**Semoga berjaya!** [Semogə berdʒaya!]
Say hi to …	**Sampaikan salam kepada …** [Sampaikan salam kepada …]

Foreign language

I don't understand.	**Saya tidak faham.** [Saya tida faham.]
Write it down, please.	**Silahkan tulis ini.** [Silahkan tulis ini.]
Do you speak ...?	**Anda boleh bercakap bahasa ...?** [Anda boleh bertʃakap bahasa ...?]
I speak a little bit of ...	**Saya bercakap sedikit bahasa ...** [Saya bertʃakap sedikit bahasa ...]
English	**Inggeris** [Iŋgeris]
Turkish	**Turki** [Turki]
Arabic	**Arab** [Arap]
French	**Perancis** [Perantʃis]
German	**Jerman** [dʒerman]
Italian	**Itali** [Itali]
Spanish	**Sepanyol** [Sepanyol]
Portuguese	**Portugis** [Portugis]
Chinese	**China** [ʃinə]
Japanese	**Jepun** [dʒepun]
Can you repeat that, please.	**Silahkan, ulangi ini.** [Silahkan, ulaŋi ini.]
I understand.	**Saya faham.** [Saya faham.]
I don't understand.	**Saya tidak faham.** [Saya tida faham.]
Please speak more slowly.	**Silahkan, cakap perlahan.** [Silahkan, tʃakap perlahan.]
Is that correct? (Am I saying it right?)	**Itu betul?** [Itu betul?]
What is this? (What does this mean?)	**Apa ini? (Perkataan apa ini?)** [Apə ini? Perkataan apə ini?]

Apologies

Excuse me, please.	**Silahkan maaf.** [Silahkan maaf.]
I'm sorry.	**Saya merasa kesal.** [Sayə merasə kesal.]
I'm really sorry.	**Saya betul-betul merasa kesal.** [Sayə betul-betul merasə kesal.]
Sorry, it's my fault.	**Maaf, itu salah saya.** [Maaf, itu salah saya.]
My mistake.	**Salah saya.** [Salah saya.]
May I ...?	**Boleh saya ...?** [Boleh saya ...?]
Do you mind if I ...?	**Anda tidak berkeberatan kalau saya ...?** [Andə tida berkeberatan kalau saya ...?]
It's OK.	**Tidak apa-apa.** [Tida apa-apa.]
It's all right.	**Segalanya OK.** [Segalanyə okej.]
Don't worry about it.	**Jangan bimbang.** [dʒaŋan bimbaŋ.]

Agreement

Yes.	**Ya** [Ya.]
Yes, sure.	**Ya, tentu.** [Ya, tentu.]
OK (Good!)	**Baik!** [Baik!]
Very well.	**Baik sekali!** [Bai sekali!]
Certainly!	**Tentu!** [Tentu!]
I agree.	**Saya setuju.** [Sayə setudʒu.]
That's correct.	**Betul.** [Betul.]
That's right.	**Betul.** [Betul.]
You're right.	**Anda betul.** [Andə betul.]
I don't mind.	**Saya tidak berkeberatan.** [Sayə tida berkeberatan.]
Absolutely right.	**Sama sekali betul.** [Samə sekali betul.]
It's possible.	**Itu mungkin.** [Itu muŋkin.]
That's a good idea.	**Itu idea baik.** [Itu ideə bai.]
I can't say no.	**Saya tidak boleh menolak.** [Sayə tida boleh menola.]
I'd be happy to.	**Saya akan senang sekali.** [Sayə akan senaŋ sekali.]
With pleasure.	**Dengan senang.** [Deŋan senaŋ.]

Refusal. Expressing doubt

No.	**Tidak.** [Tida.]
Certainly not.	**Tentu tidak.** [Tentu tida.]
I don't agree.	**Saya tidak setuju.** [Sayə tida setudʒu.]
I don't think so.	**Saya tidak fikir begitu.** [Sayə tida fikir begitu.]
It's not true.	**Itu tidak betul.** [Itu tida betul.]
You are wrong.	**Anda tidak betul.** [Andə tida betul.]
I think you are wrong.	**Saya fikir anda tidak betul.** [Sayə fikir andə tida betul.]
I'm not sure.	**Saya ragu-ragu.** [Sayə ragu-ragu.]
It's impossible.	**Itu mustahil.** [Itu mustahil.]
Nothing of the kind (sort)!	**Sama sekali tidak!** [Samə sekali tidak!]
The exact opposite.	**Sebaliknya!** [Sebaliknya!]
I'm against it.	**Saya berkeberatan.** [Sayə berkeberatan.]
I don't care.	**Untuk saya sama saja.** [Untu sayə samə sadʒa.]
I have no idea.	**Saya tidak tahu-menahu.** [Sayə tida tahu-menahu.]
I doubt it.	**Ragu-ragu itu.** [Ragu-ragu itu.]
Sorry, I can't.	**Maaf saya tidak boleh.** [Maaf sayə tida boleh.]
Sorry, I don't want to.	**Maaf, saya tidak mahu.** [Maaf, sayə tida mahu.]
Thank you, but I don't need this.	**Terima kasih, saya tidak memerlukan itu.** [Terimə kasih, sayə tida memerlukan itu.]
It's getting late.	**Sudah larut malam.** [Sudah larut malam.]

I have to get up early.

Saya harus bangun pagi-pagi.
[Sayə harus baŋun pagi-pagi.]

I don't feel well.

Saya kurang enak badan.
[Sayə kuraŋ ena badan.]

Expressing gratitude

Thank you. | **Terima kasih.**
[Terimə kasih.]

Thank you very much. | **Terima kasih banyak.**
[Terimə kasih banya.]

I really appreciate it. | **Saya sangat bersyukur.**
[Sayə saŋat berçukur.]

I'm really grateful to you. | **Saya sangat berterima kasih kepada anda.**
[Sayə saŋat berterimə kasih kepadə anda.]

We are really grateful to you. | **Kami sangat berterima kasih kepada anda.**
[Kami saŋat berterimə kasih kepadə anda.]

Thank you for your time. | **Terima kasih kerana menghabiskan masa.**
[Terimə kasih keranə menɣabiskan masa.]

Thanks for everything. | **Terima kasih atas segalanya.**
[Terimə kasih atas segalanya.]

Thank you for ... | **Terima kasih atas ...**
[Terimə kasih atas ...]

your help | **bantuan anda**
[bantuan andə]

a nice time | **masa yang baik**
[masə yaŋ bai]

a wonderful meal | **makanan yang sedap**
[makanan yaŋ sedap]

a pleasant evening | **malam yang indah**
[malam yaŋ indah]

a wonderful day | **hari yang menyenangkan**
[hari yaŋ menyenaŋkan]

an amazing journey | **darmawisata yang seronok**
[darmawisatə yaŋ serono]

Don't mention it. | **Sama-sama.**
[Sama-sama.]

You are welcome. | **Sama-sama.**
[Sama-sama.]

Any time. | **Selalu sedia.**
[Selalu sedia.]

My pleasure. | **Saya senang membantu.**
[Sayə senaŋ membantu.]

Forget it.

Lupakan saja. Segalanya OK.
[Lupakan saʤa. Segalanyə okej.]

Don't worry about it.

Jangan susah.
[dʒaŋan susah.]

Congratulations. Best wishes

Congratulations!	**Tahniah!** [Tahniah!]
Happy birthday!	**Selamat Hari Jadi!** [Selamat Hari ʤadi!]
Merry Christmas!	**Selamat Hari Krismas!** [Selamat Hari Krismas!]
Happy New Year!	**Selamat Tahun Baru!** [Selamat Tahun Baru!]
Happy Easter!	**Selamat Hari Easter!** [Selamat Hari Easter!]
Happy Hanukkah!	**Selamat Hanukkah!** [Selamat Hanukka!]
I'd like to propose a toast.	**Saya nak mengajukan minum ucap selamat.** [Sayə na meŋaʤukan minum uʧap selamat.]
Cheers!	**Untuk kesihatan anda!** [Untu kesihatan anda!]
Let's drink to …!	**Mari minum untuk kesihatan …!** [Mari minum untu kesihatan …!]
To our success!	**Untuk kejayaan kita!** [Untu keʤayaan kita!]
To your success!	**Untuk kejayaan anda!** [Untu keʤayaan anda!]
Good luck!	**Selamat berjaya!** [Selamat berʤaya!]
Have a nice day!	**Semoga hari anda baik sahaja!** [Semogə hari andə bai sahaʤa!]
Have a good holiday!	**Selamat berehat!** [Selamat berehat!]
Have a safe journey!	**Selamat jalan!** [Selamat ʤalan!]
I hope you get better soon!	**Semoga anda cepat sembuh!** [Semogə andə ʧepat sembuh!]

Socializing

Why are you sad?

Mengapa anda sedih?
[Meɳapə andə sedih?]

Smile! Cheer up!

Senyumlah!
[Senyumlah!]

Are you free tonight?

Anda ada lapang malam ini?
[Andə adə lapaɳ malam ini?]

May I offer you a drink?

Boleh saya menawarkan anda minum sesuatu?
[Boleh sayə menawarkan andə minum sesuatu?]

Would you like to dance?

Mahu menari?
[Mahu menari?]

Let's go to the movies.

Mari pergi tengok filem.
[Mari pergi teɳo filem.]

May I invite you to …?

Boleh saya mempelawa anda ke …?
[Boleh sayə mempelawə andə ke …?]

a restaurant

restoran
[restoran]

the movies

pawagam
[pawagam]

the theater

teater
[teater]

go for a walk

berjalan-jalan
[berdʒalan-dʒalan]

At what time?

Pukul berapa?
[Pukul berapa?]

tonight

malam ini
[malam ini]

at six

pukul enam
[pukul enam]

at seven

pukul tujuh
[pukul tudʒuh]

at eight

pukul lapan
[pukul lapan]

at nine

pukul sembilan
[pukul sembilan]

Do you like it here?

Anda suka di sini?
[Andǝ sukǝ di sini?]

Are you here with someone?

Anda di sini bersama dengan seseorang?
[Andǝ di sini bersamǝ deŋan seseoraŋ?]

I'm with my friend.

Saya bersama dengan teman/ teman wanita.
[Sayǝ bersamǝ deŋan teman/ teman wanita.]

I'm with my friends.

Saya bersama dengan kawan-kawan.
[Sayǝ bersamǝ deŋan kawan-kawan.]

No, I'm alone.

Saya seorang diri.
[Sayǝ seoraŋ diri.]

Do you have a boyfriend?

Awak ada sahabat?
[Awa adǝ sahabat?]

I have a boyfriend.

Saya ada sahabat.
[Sayǝ adǝ sahabat.]

Do you have a girlfriend?

Awak ada teman wanita?
[Awa adǝ teman wanita?]

I have a girlfriend.

Saya ada teman wanita.
[Sayǝ adǝ teman wanita.]

Can I see you again?

Kita akan berjumpa lagi?
[Kitǝ akan berdʒumpǝ lagi?]

Can I call you?

Boleh saya telefon kepada awak?
[Boleh sayǝ telefon kepadǝ awak?]

Call me. (Give me a call.)

Telefon kepada saya.
[Telefon kepadǝ saya.]

What's your number?

Nombor berapa telefon awak?
[Nombor berapǝ telefon awak?]

I miss you.

Saya rindu awak.
[Sayǝ rindu awa.]

You have a beautiful name.

Nama anda sangat cantik.
[Namǝ andǝ saŋat tʃanti.]

I love you.

Saya cinta padamu.
[Sayǝ tʃintǝ padamu.]

Will you marry me?

Kahwinlah saya.
[Kahwinlah saya.]

You're kidding!

Anda bergurau!
[Andǝ bergurau!]

I'm just kidding.

Saya bergurau saja.
[Sayǝ bergurau sadʒa.]

Are you serious?

Anda serius?
[Andǝ serius?]

I'm serious.

Saya serius.
[Sayǝ serius.]

Really?!

Betulkah?!
[Betulkah?!]

It's unbelievable!

Sukar dipercayai!
[Sukar dipertʃayai!]

I don't believe you.

Saya tidak percaya kepada anda.
[Sayə tida pertʃayə kepadə anda.]

I can't.

Saya tidak boleh.
[Sayə tida boleh.]

I don't know.

Saya tidak tahu.
[Sayə tida tahu.]

I don't understand you.

Saya tidak memahami anda.
[Sayə tida memahami anda.]

Please go away.

Silahkan pergi.
[Silahkan pergi.]

Leave me alone!

Tinggalkan saya!
[Tiŋgalkan saya!]

I can't stand him.

Saya membencinya.
[Sayə membentʃinya.]

You are disgusting!

Anda jijik!
[Andə dʒidʒik!]

I'll call the police!

Saya akan panggil polis!
[Sayə akan paŋgil polis!]

Sharing impressions. Emotions

I like it.	**Saya suka ini.** [Sayə sukə ini.]
Very nice.	**Sangat elok.** [Saŋat elo.]
That's great!	**Ini hebat!** [Ini hebat!]
It's not bad.	**Ini agak baik.** [Ini agə bai.]
I don't like it.	**Saya tidak suka ini.** [Sayə tidə sukə ini.]
It's not good.	**Ini kurang baik.** [Ini kuraŋ bai.]
It's bad.	**Ini buruk.** [Ini buru.]
It's very bad.	**Ini buruk sekali.** [Ini buru sekali.]
It's disgusting.	**Ini jijik.** [Ini dʒidʒi.]
I'm happy.	**Saya berbahagia.** [Sayə berbahagia.]
I'm content.	**Saya puas.** [Sayə puas.]
I'm in love.	**Saya jatuh cinta.** [Sayə dʒatuh tʃinta.]
I'm calm.	**Saya tenang.** [Sayə tenaŋ.]
I'm bored.	**Saya merasa bosan.** [Sayə merasə bosan.]
I'm tired.	**Saya letih.** [Sayə letih.]
I'm sad.	**Saya sedih.** [Sayə sedih.]
I'm frightened.	**Saya takut.** [Sayə takut.]
I'm angry.	**Saya marah.** [Sayə marah.]
I'm worried.	**Saya khuatir.** [Sayə χuatir.]
I'm nervous.	**Saya gementar.** [Sayə gementar.]

I'm jealous. (envious)

Saya cemburu.
[Sayə tʃemburu.]

I'm surprised.

Saya hairan.
[Sayə hairan.]

I'm perplexed.

Saya bingung.
[Sayə biŋuŋ.]

Problems. Accidents

I've got a problem.	**Saya ada masalah.** [Sayə adə masalah.]
We've got a problem.	**Kami ada masalah.** [Kami adə masalah.]
I'm lost.	**Saya sesat jalan.** [Sayə sesat dʒalan.]
I missed the last bus (train).	**Saya tertinggal bas yang terakhir.** [Sayə tertiŋgal bas yaŋ teraχir.]
I don't have any money left.	**Saya menghabiskan segala wang.** [Sayə menɣabiskan segalə waŋ.]
I've lost my ...	**Saya kehilangan ...** [Sayə kehilaŋan ...]
Someone stole my ...	**Saya kecurian ...** [Sayə ketʃurian ...]
passport	**pasport** [pasport]
wallet	**dompet** [dompet]
papers	**kad pengenalan** [kat peŋenalan]
ticket	**tiket** [tiket]
money	**wang** [waŋ]
handbag	**beg** [beg]
camera	**kamera** [kamerə]
laptop	**komputer riba** [komputer ribə]
tablet computer	**komputer tablet** [komputer tablet]
mobile phone	**telefon bimbit** [telefon bimbit]
Help me!	**Tolong!** [T:oloŋ!]
What's happened?	**Apa terjadi?** [Apə terdʒadi?]
fire	**kebakaran** [kebakaran]

shooting	**tembakan** [tembakan]
murder	**pembunuhan** [pembunuhan]
explosion	**ledakan** [ledakan]
fight	**perkelahian** [perkelahian]

Call the police!	**Panggil polis!** [Paŋgil polis!]
Please hurry up!	**Silahkan, cepat!** [Silahkan, tʃepat!]
I'm looking for the police station.	**Saya cari balai polis.** [Sayə tʃari balai polis.]
I need to make a call.	**Saya perlu telefon.** [Sayə perlu telefon.]
May I use your phone?	**Boleh saya telefon?** [Boleh sayə telefon?]

I've been …	**Saya …** [Sayə …]
mugged	**dirompak** [dirompa]
robbed	**kecurian** [ketʃurian]
raped	**diperkosa** [diperkosə]
attacked (beaten up)	**dipukul** [dipukul]

Are you all right?	**Anda OK?** [Andə okej?]
Did you see who it was?	**Anda melihat, siapa tadi itu?** [Andə melihat, siapə tadi itu?]
Would you be able to recognize the person?	**Anda boleh mengenalinya?** [Andə boleh meŋenalinya?]
Are you sure?	**Anda benar-benar pasti?** [Andə benar-benar pasti?]
Please calm down.	**Silahkan tenang.** [Silahkan tenaŋ.]
Take it easy!	**Jangan ambil berat!** [dʒaŋan ambil berat!]
Don't worry!	**Jangan khuatir.** [dʒaŋan χuatir.]
Everything will be fine.	**Segalanya akan berakhir baik.** [Segalanyə akan beraχir bai.]
Everything's all right.	**Segalanya OK.** [Segalanyə okej.]
Come here, please.	**Silahkan datang ke sini.** [Silahkan dataŋ ke sini.]

I have some questions for you. **Saya ada beberapa soalan untuk anda.**
[Sayə adə beberapə soalan untu anda.]

Wait a moment, please. **Tolong tunggu sekejap.**
[Toloŋ tuŋgu sekedʒap.]

Do you have any I.D.? **Anda ada kad pengenalan?**
[Andə adə kat peŋenalan?]

Thanks. You can leave now. **Terima kasih. Anda boleh pergi.**
[Terimə kasih. Andə boleh pergi.]

Hands behind your head! **Tangan ke belakang kepala!**
[Taŋan ke belakaŋ kepala!]

You're under arrest! **Anda ditangkap!**
[Andə ditaŋkap!]

Health problems

Please help me.	**Silahkan tolong.** [Silahkan toloŋ.]
I don't feel well.	**Saya kurang sihat.** [Sayə kuraŋ sihat.]
My husband doesn't feel well.	**Suami saya kurang sihat.** [Suami sayə kuraŋ sihat.]
My son ...	**Anak lelaki saya ...** [Ana lelaki sayə ...]
My father ...	**Bapa saya ...** [Bapə sayə ...]
My wife doesn't feel well.	**Isteri saya kurang sihat.** [Isteri sayə kuraŋ sihat.]
My daughter ...	**Anak perempuan saya ...** [Ana perempuan sayə ...]
My mother ...	**Ibu saya ...** [Ibu sayə ...]
I've got a ...	**... saya sakit.** [... sayə sakit.]
headache	**kepala** [kepalə]
sore throat	**tekak** [teka]
stomach ache	**perut** [perut]
toothache	**gigi** [gigi]
I feel dizzy.	**Kepala saya pusing.** [Kepalə sayə pusiŋ.]
He has a fever.	**Dia demam.** [Diə demam.]
She has a fever.	**Dia demam.** [Diə demam.]
I can't breathe.	**Saya susah nafas.** [Sayə susah nafas.]
I'm short of breath.	**Saya semput.** [Sayə semput.]
I am asthmatic.	**Saya mengidap sakit lelah.** [Sayə meɲidap sakit lelah.]
I am diabetic.	**Saya mengidap diabetis.** [Sayə meɲidap diabetis.]

I can't sleep.	**Saya kurang tidur.** [Sayə kuraŋ tidur.]
food poisoning	**keracunan makanan** [keratʃunan makanan]

It hurts here.	**Sakit di sini.** [Sakit di sini.]
Help me!	**Tolong!** [Toloŋ!]
I am here!	**Saya di sini!** [Sayə di sini!]
We are here!	**Kami di sini!** [Kami di sini!]
Get me out of here!	**Keluarkan saya dari sini!** [Keluarkan sayə dari sini!]
I need a doctor.	**Saya perlukan doktor.** [Sayə perlukan doktor.]
I can't move.	**Saya tidak boleh bergerak.** [Sayə tida boleh bergera.]
I can't move my legs.	**Saya tidak boleh menggerakkan kaki.** [Sayə tida boleh meŋgerakkan kaki.]

I have a wound.	**Saya cedera.** [Sayə tʃedera.]
Is it serious?	**Adakah itu serius?** [Adakah itu serius?]
My documents are in my pocket.	**Kad pengenalan saya di dalam saku.** [Kat peŋenalan sayə di dalam saku.]
Calm down!	**Tenang saja!** [Tenaŋ sadʒa!]
May I use your phone?	**Boleh saya telefon?** [Boleh sayə telefon?]

Call an ambulance!	**Panggil ambulans!** [Paŋgil ambulans!]
It's urgent!	**Itu segera!** [Itu segera!]
It's an emergency!	**Itu sangat segera!** [Itu saŋat segera!]
Please hurry up!	**Silahkan, segera!** [Silahkan, segera!]
Would you please call a doctor?	**Silahkan panggil doktor.** [Silahkan paŋgil doktor.]
Where is the hospital?	**Beritahulah, di mana hospital.** [Beritahulah, di manə hospital.]

How are you feeling?	**Bagaimana anda rasa?** [Bagaimanə andə rasa?]
Are you all right?	**Segalanya OK dengan anda?** [Segalanyə okej deŋan anda?]
What's happened?	**Apa terjadi?** [Apə terdʒadi?]

I feel better now.

Saya sudah merasa lebih baik.
[Saya sudah merasa lebih bai.]

It's OK.

Segalanya beres.
[Segalanya beres.]

It's all right.

Segalanya baik.
[Segalanya bai.]

At the pharmacy

pharmacy (drugstore)	**kedai ubat** [kedai ubat]
24-hour pharmacy	**kedai ubat 24 jam** [kedai ubat dua puluh empat dʒam]
Where is the closest pharmacy?	**Di mada kedai ubat terdekat?** [Di madə kedai ubat terdekat?]
Is it open now?	**Ia sekarang buka?** [Iə sekaraŋ buka?]
At what time does it open?	**Pukul berapa ia buka?** [Pukul berapə iə buka?]
At what time does it close?	**Sampai pukul berapa ia buka?** [Sampai pukul berapə iə buka?]
Is it far?	**Ini jauh?** [Ini dʒauh?]
Can I get there on foot?	**Boleh saya sampai ke situ dengan berjalan kaki?** [Boleh sayə sampai ke situ deŋan berdʒalan kaki?]
Can you show me on the map?	**Silahkan tunjukkan di peta.** [Silahkan tundʒukkan di peta.]
Please give me something for ...	**Bagi saya sesuatu untuk ...** [Bagi sayə sesuatu untu ...]
a headache	**sakit kepala** [sakit kepalə]
a cough	**batuk** [batu]
a cold	**masuk angin** [masu aŋin]
the flu	**selesema** [seleseme]
a fever	**demam** [demam]
a stomach ache	**sakit gaster** [sakit gaster]
nausea	**muntah** [muntah]
diarrhea	**cirit-birit** [tʃirit-birit]
constipation	**konstipasi** [konstipasi]

pain in the back	**sakit di belakang** [sakit di belakaŋ]
chest pain	**sakit di dada** [sakit di dadə]
side stitch	**sakit di rusuk** [sakit di rusu]
abdominal pain	**sakit perut** [sakit perut]

pill	**pil** [pil]
ointment, cream	**salep** [salep]
syrup	**sirap** [sirap]
spray	**penyembur** [penyembur]
drops	**tetes** [tetes]

You need to go to the hospital.	**Anda perlu pergi ke hospital.** [Andə perlu pergi ke hospital.]
health insurance	**insurans** [insurans]
prescription	**preskripsi** [preskripsi]
insect repellant	**penghalau serangga** [penɣalau seraŋgə]
Band Aid	**plaster** [plaster]

The bare minimum

Excuse me, …	**Maaf, …** [Maaf, …]
Hello.	**Salam sejahtera.** [Salam sedʒahtera.]
Thank you.	**Terima kasih.** [Terimə kasih.]
Good bye.	**Sampai jumpa lagi.** [Sampai dʒumpə lagi.]
Yes.	**Ya.** [Ya.]
No.	**Tidak.** [Tida.]
I don't know.	**Saya tidak tahu.** [Sayə tida tahu.]
Where? | Where to? | When?	**Di mana? | Ke mana? | Bila?** [Di mana? | Ke mana? | Bila?]
I need …	**Saya perlukan …** [Sayə perlukan …]
I want …	**Saya mahu …** [Sayə mahu …]
Do you have ...?	**Anda ada ...?** [Andə ada ...?]
Is there a … here?	**Di sini ada ...?** [Di sini ada ...?]
May I …?	**Boleh saya ...?** [Boleh saya ...?]
…, please (polite request)	**Silahkan** [Silahkan]
I'm looking for …	**Saya cari …** [Sayə tʃari …]
the restroom	**tandas** [tandas]
an ATM	**ATM** [ateem]
a pharmacy (drugstore)	**kedai ubat** [kedai ubat]
a hospital	**hospital** [hospital]
the police station	**balai polis** [balai polis]
the subway	**LRT** [elerte]

a taxi	**teksi** [teksi]
the train station	**stesen kereta api** [stesen keretə api]

My name is …	**Nama saya …** [Namə saya …]
What's your name?	**Siapa nama anda?** [Siapə namə anda?]
Could you please help me?	**Silahkan tolong saya.** [Silahkan toloŋ saya.]
I've got a problem.	**Saya ada masalah.** [Sayə adə masalah.]
I don't feel well.	**Saya kurang enak badan.** [Sayə kuraŋ ena badan.]
Call an ambulance!	**Tolong panggil ambulans!** [Toloŋ paŋgil ambulans!]
May I make a call?	**Boleh saya telefon?** [Boleh sayə telefon?]

I'm sorry.	**Maaf** [Maaf]
You're welcome.	**Sama-sama** [Sama-samə]

I, me	**saya** [sayə]
you (inform.)	**awak** [awa]
he	**dia** [diə]
she	**dia** [diə]
they (masc.)	**mereka** [merekə]
they (fem.)	**mereka** [merekə]
we	**kita, kami** [kita, kami]
you (pl)	**kamu sekalian** [kamu sekalian]
you (sg, form.)	**Anda** [Andə]

ENTRANCE	**MASUK** [masu]
EXIT	**keluar** [keluar]
OUT OF ORDER	**rosak** [rosa]
CLOSED	**tutup** [tutup]

OPEN

BUKA
[bukə]

FOR WOMEN

untuk perempuan
[untu perempuan]

FOR MEN

untuk lelaki
[untu lelaki]

TOPICAL
VOCABULARY

This section contains more than 3,000 of the most important words.
The dictionary will provide invaluable assistance while traveling abroad, because frequently individual words are enough for you to be understood.
The dictionary includes a convenient transcription of each foreign word

T&P Books Publishing

VOCABULARY CONTENTS

T&P Books Publishing

BASIC CONCEPTS

T&P Books Publishing

1. Pronouns

I, me	**saya, aku**	[sajə], [aku]
you	**awak**	[ava]
he, she, it	**dia, ia**	[diə], [ia]
we	**kami, kita**	[kami], [kitə]
you (to a group)	**kamu**	[kamu]
you (polite, sing.)	**anda**	[andə]
you (polite, pl)	**anda**	[andə]
they (inanim.)	**ia**	[ia]
they (anim.)	**mereka**	[mɛrekə]

2. Greetings. Salutations

Hello! (fam.)	**Helo!**	[helo]
Hello! (form.)	**Helo!**	[helo]
Good morning!	**Selamat pagi!**	[sɛlamat pagi]
Good afternoon!	**Selamat petang!**	[sɛlamat pɛtaŋ]
Good evening!	**Selamat petang!**	[sɛlamat pɛtaŋ]
to say hello	**bersapa**	[bɛrsapə]
Hi! (hello)	**Hai!**	[haj]
greeting (n)	**sambutan**	[sambutan]
to greet (vt)	**menyambut**	[mɛnjambut]
How are you?	**Apa khabar?**	[apa kabar]
What's new?	**Apa yang baru?**	[apa jaŋ baru]
Bye-Bye! Goodbye!	**Sampai jumpa lagi!**	[sampaj dʒumpa lagi]
See you soon!	**Sampai jumpa lagi!**	[sampaj dʒumpa lagi]
Farewell!	**Selamat tinggal!**	[sɛlamat tiŋgal]
to say goodbye	**minta diri**	[minta diri]
So long!	**Jumpa lagi!**	[dʒumpa lagi]
Thank you!	**Terima kasih!**	[tɛrima kasih]
Thank you very much!	**Terima kasih banyak!**	[tɛrima kasih banjak]
You're welcome	**Sama-sama**	[sama samə]
Don't mention it!	**Sama-sama!**	[sama samə]
It was nothing	**Sama-sama**	[sama samə]
Excuse me! (fam.)	**Maaf!**	[maaf]
Excuse me! (form.)	**Minta maaf!**	[minta maaf]
to excuse (forgive)	**memaafkan**	[mɛmaafkan]

to apologize (vi)	minta maaf	[minta maaf]
My apologies	Maafkan saya	[maafkan sajə]
I'm sorry!	Maaf!	[maaf]
to forgive (vt)	memaafkan	[mɛmaafkan]
It's okay! (that's all right)	Tidak apa-apa!	[tidak apa apə]
please (adv)	sila, tolong	[silə], [toloŋ]
Don't forget!	Jangan lupa!	[dʒaŋan lupə]
Certainly!	Tentu!	[tɛntu]
Of course not!	Tentu tidak!	[tɛntu tidak]
Okay! (I agree)	Setuju!	[sɛtudʒu]
That's enough!	Cukuplah!	[tʃukuplah]

3. Questions

Who?	Siapa?	[siapə]
What?	Apa?	[apə]
Where? (at, in)	Di mana?	[di manə]
Where (to)?	Ke mana?	[kɛ manə]
From where?	Dari mana?	[dari manə]
When?	Bila?	[bilə]
Why? (What for?)	Untuk apa?	[untuk apə]
Why? (~ are you crying?)	Mengapa?	[mɛŋapə]
What for?	Untuk apa?	[untuk apə]
How? (in what way)	Bagaimana?	[bagajmanə]
What? (What kind of ...?)	Apa? Yang mana?	[apə], [jaŋ manə]
Which?	Yang mana?	[jaŋ manə]
To whom?	Kepada siapa?	[kɛpada siapə]
About whom?	Tentang siapa?	[tɛntaŋ siapə]
About what?	Tentang apa?	[tɛntaŋ apə]
With whom?	Dengan siapa?	[dɛŋan siapə]
How many? How much?	Berapa?	[brapə]
Whose?	Siapa punya?	[siapa punjə]

4. Prepositions

with (accompanied by)	bersama dengan	[bɛrsama dɛŋan]
without	tanpa	[tanpə]
to (indicating direction)	ke	[kɛ]
about (talking ~ ...)	tentang	[tɛntaŋ]
before (in time)	sebelum	[sɛbɛlum]
in front of ...	di depan	[di dɛpan]
under (beneath, below)	di bawah	[di bavah]
above (over)	di atas	[di atas]

on (atop)	**di atas**	[di atas]
from (off, out of)	**dari**	[dari]
of (made from)	**daripada**	[daripadə]
in (e.g., ~ ten minutes)	**selepas**	[sɛlɛpas]
over (across the top of)	**melalui**	[mɛlalui]

5. Function words. Adverbs. Part 1

Where? (at, in)	**Di mana?**	[di manə]
here (adv)	**di sini**	[di sini]
there (adv)	**di situ**	[di situ]
somewhere (to be)	**pada sesuatu tempat**	[pada sɛsuatu tɛmpat]
nowhere (not in any place)	**tak di mana-mana**	[tak di mana manə]
by (near, beside)	**dekat, kat**	[dɛkat], [kat]
by the window	**kat tingkap**	[kat tiŋkap]
Where (to)?	**Ke mana?**	[kɛ manə]
here (e.g., come ~!)	**ke sini**	[kɛ sini]
there (e.g., to go ~)	**ke situ**	[kɛ situ]
from here (adv)	**dari sini**	[dari sini]
from there (adv)	**dari situ**	[dari situ]
close (adv)	**dekat**	[dɛkat]
far (adv)	**jauh**	[dʒauh]
near (e.g., ~ Paris)	**dekat**	[dɛkat]
nearby (adv)	**dekat**	[dɛkat]
not far (adv)	**tidak jauh**	[tidak dʒauh]
left (adj)	**kiri**	[kiri]
on the left	**di kiri**	[di kiri]
to the left	**ke kiri**	[kɛ kiri]
right (adj)	**kanan**	[kanan]
on the right	**di kanan**	[di kanan]
to the right	**ke kanan**	[kɛ kanan]
in front (adv)	**di depan**	[di dɛpan]
front (as adj)	**depan**	[dɛpan]
ahead (the kids ran ~)	**ke depan**	[kɛ dɛpan]
behind (adv)	**di belakang**	[di blakaŋ]
from behind	**dari belakang**	[dari blakaŋ]
back (towards the rear)	**mundur**	[mundur]
middle	**tengah**	[tɛŋah]
in the middle	**di tengah**	[di tɛŋah]

at the side	dari sisi	[dari sisi]
everywhere (adv)	di mana-mana	[di mana manə]
around (in all directions)	di sekitar	[di sɛkitar]

from inside	dari dalam	[dari dalam]
somewhere (to go)	entah ke mana	[ɛntah kɛ manə]
straight (directly)	terus	[trus]
back (e.g., come ~)	balik	[bali]

| from anywhere | dari sesuatu tempat | [dari sɛsuatu tɛmpat] |
| from somewhere | entah dari mana | [ɛntah dari manə] |

firstly (adv)	pertama	[pɛrtamə]
secondly (adv)	kedua	[kɛduə]
thirdly (adv)	ketiga	[kɛtigə]

suddenly (adv)	tiba-tiba	[tiba tibə]
at first (in the beginning)	mula-mula	[mula mulə]
for the first time	pertama kali	[pɛrtama kali]
long before ...	lama sebelum	[lama sɛbɛlum]
anew (over again)	semula	[sɛmulə]
for good (adv)	untuk selama-lamanya	[untuk sɛlama lamanjə]

never (adv)	tidak sekali-kali	[tidak sɛkali kali]
again (adv)	lagi, semula	[lagi], [sɛmulə]
now (at present)	sekarang, kini	[sɛkaraŋ], [kini]
often (adv)	seringkali	[sɛriŋkali]
then (adv)	ketika itu	[kɛtika itu]
urgently (quickly)	segera	[sɛgɛrə]
usually (adv)	biasanya	[bijasanjə]

by the way, ...	oh ya	[o jə]
possibly	mungkin	[muŋkin]
probably (adv)	mungkin	[muŋkin]
maybe (adv)	mungkin	[muŋkin]
besides ...	selain itu	[sɛlajn itu]
that's why ...	kerana itu	[krana itu]
in spite of ...	meskipun	[mɛskipun]
thanks to ...	berkat	[bɛrkat]

what (pron.)	apa	[apə]
that (conj.)	bahawa	[bahvə]
something	sesuatu	[sɛsuatu]
anything (something)	sesuatu	[sɛsuatu]
nothing	tidak apa-apa	[tidak apa apə]

who (pron.)	siapa	[siapə]
someone	seseorang	[sɛsɛoraŋ]
somebody	seseorang	[sɛsɛoraŋ]

| nobody | tak seorang pun | [tak sɛoraŋ pun] |
| nowhere (a voyage to ~) | tak ke mana pun | [tak ke mana pun] |

nobody's	**tak bertuan**	[tak bɛrtuan]
somebody's	**milik seseorang**	[milik sɛsɛoraŋ]
so (I'm ~ glad)	**begitu**	[bɛgitu]
also (as well)	**juga**	[dʒugə]
too (as well)	**juga**	[dʒugə]

6. Function words. Adverbs. Part 2

Why?	**Mengapa?**	[mɛŋapə]
for some reason	**entah mengapa**	[ɛntah meŋapə]
because …	**oleh kerana**	[oleh kranə]
for some purpose	**entah untuk apa**	[ɛntah untuk apə]
and	**dan**	[dan]
or	**atau**	[atau]
but	**tetapi**	[tɛtapi]
for (e.g., ~ me)	**untuk**	[untu]
too (~ many people)	**terlalu**	[tɛrlalu]
only (exclusively)	**hanya**	[hanjə]
exactly (adv)	**tepat**	[tɛpat]
about (more or less)	**sekitar**	[sɛkitar]
approximately (adv)	**lebih kurang**	[lɛbih kuraŋ]
approximate (adj)	**lebih kurang**	[lɛbih kuraŋ]
almost (adv)	**hampir**	[hampir]
the rest	**yang lain**	[jaŋ lajn]
the other (second)	**kedua**	[kɛduə]
other (different)	**lain**	[lajn]
each (adj)	**setiap**	[sɛtiap]
any (no matter which)	**sebarang**	[sɛbaraŋ]
many, much (a lot of)	**ramai, banyak**	[ramaj], [banjə]
many people	**ramai orang**	[ramaj oraŋ]
all (everyone)	**semua**	[sɛmuə]
in return for …	**sebagai pertukaran untuk**	[sɛbagaj pɛrtukaran untu]
in exchange (adv)	**sebagai tukaran**	[sɛbagaj tukaran]
by hand (made)	**dengan tangan**	[dɛŋan taŋan]
hardly (negative opinion)	**mustahil**	[mustahil]
probably (adv)	**mungkin**	[muŋkin]
on purpose (intentionally)	**sengaja**	[sɛŋadʒə]
by accident (adv)	**tidak sengaja**	[tidak sɛŋadʒə]
very (adv)	**sangat**	[saŋat]
for example (adv)	**misalnya**	[misalnjə]
between	**antara**	[antɑrə]

among	**di antara**	[di antarə]
so much (such a lot)	**seberapa ini**	[sɛbrapa ini]
especially (adv)	**terutama**	[tɛrutamə]

NUMBERS.
MISCELLANEOUS

T&P Books Publishing

7. Cardinal numbers. Part 1

0 zero	**sifar**	[sifar]
1 one	**satu**	[satu]
2 two	**dua**	[duə]
3 three	**tiga**	[tigə]
4 four	**empat**	[ɛmpat]
5 five	**lima**	[limə]
6 six	**enam**	[ɛnam]
7 seven	**tujuh**	[tuʤuh]
8 eight	**lapan**	[lapan]
9 nine	**sembilan**	[sɛmbilan]
10 ten	**sepuluh**	[sɛpuluh]
11 eleven	**sebelas**	[sɛblas]
12 twelve	**dua belas**	[dua blas]
13 thirteen	**tiga belas**	[tiga blas]
14 fourteen	**empat belas**	[ɛmpat blas]
15 fifteen	**lima belas**	[lima blas]
16 sixteen	**enam belas**	[ɛnam blas]
17 seventeen	**tujuh belas**	[tuʤuh blas]
18 eighteen	**lapan belas**	[lapan blas]
19 nineteen	**sembilan belas**	[sɛmbilan blas]
20 twenty	**dua puluh**	[dua puluh]
21 twenty-one	**dua puluh satu**	[dua puluh satu]
22 twenty-two	**dua puluh dua**	[dua puluh duə]
23 twenty-three	**dua puluh tiga**	[dua puluh tigə]
30 thirty	**tiga puluh**	[tiga puluh]
31 thirty-one	**tiga puluh satu**	[tiga puluh satu]
32 thirty-two	**tiga puluh dua**	[tiga puluh duə]
33 thirty-three	**tiga puluh tiga**	[tiga puluh tigə]
40 forty	**empat puluh**	[ɛmpat puluh]
41 forty-one	**empat puluh satu**	[ɛmpat puluh satu]
42 forty-two	**empat puluh dua**	[ɛmpat puluh duə]
43 forty-three	**empat puluh tiga**	[ɛmpat puluh tigə]
50 fifty	**lima puluh**	[lima puluh]
51 fifty-one	**lima puluh satu**	[lima puluh satu]
52 fifty-two	**lima puluh dua**	[lima puluh duə]
53 fifty-three	**lima puluh tiga**	[lima puluh tigə]
60 sixty	**enam puluh**	[ɛnam puluh]

61 sixty-one	enam puluh satu	[ɛnam puluh satu]
62 sixty-two	enam puluh dua	[ɛnam puluh duə]
63 sixty-three	enam puluh tiga	[ɛnam puluh tigə]
70 seventy	tujuh puluh	[tudʒuh puluh]
71 seventy-one	tujuh puluh satu	[tudʒuh puluh satu]
72 seventy-two	tujuh puluh dua	[tudʒuh puluh duə]
73 seventy-three	tujuh puluh tiga	[tudʒuh puluh tigə]
80 eighty	lapan puluh	[lapan puluh]
81 eighty-one	lapan puluh satu	[lapan puluh satu]
82 eighty-two	lapan puluh dua	[lapan puluh duə]
83 eighty-three	lapan puluh tiga	[lapan puluh tigə]
90 ninety	sembilan puluh	[sɛmbilan puluh]
91 ninety-one	sembulan puluh satu	[sɛmbulan puluh satu]
92 ninety-two	sembilan puluh dua	[sɛmbilan puluh duə]
93 ninety-three	sembilan puluh tiga	[ɛembilan puluh tigə]

8. Cardinal numbers. Part 2

100 one hundred	seratus	[sɛratus]
200 two hundred	dua ratus	[dua ratus]
300 three hundred	tiga ratus	[tiga ratus]
400 four hundred	empat ratus	[ɛmpat ratus]
500 five hundred	lima ratus	[lima ratus]
600 six hundred	enam ratus	[ɛnam ratus]
700 seven hundred	tujuh ratus	[tudʒuh ratus]
800 eight hundred	lapan ratus	[lapan ratus]
900 nine hundred	sembilan ratus	[sɛmbilan ratus]
1000 one thousand	seribu	[sɛribu]
2000 two thousand	dua ribu	[dua ribu]
3000 three thousand	tiga ribu	[tiga ribu]
10000 ten thousand	sepuluh ribu	[sɛpuluh ribu]
one hundred thousand	seratus ribu	[sɛratus ribu]
million	juta	[dʒutə]
billion	billion	[billion]

9. Ordinal numbers

first (adj)	pertama	[pɛrtamə]
second (adj)	kedua	[kɛduə]
third (adj)	ketiga	[kɛtigə]
fourth (adj)	keempat	[kɛɛmpat]
fifth (adj)	kelima	[kɛlimə]
sixth (adj)	keenam	[kɛɛnam]

seventh (adj)	**ketujuh**	[kɛtuʤuh]
eighth (adj)	**kelapan**	[kɛlapan]
ninth (adj)	**kesembilan**	[kɛsɛmbilan]
tenth (adj)	**kesepuluh**	[kɛsɛpuluh]

COLOURS. UNITS OF MEASUREMENT

T&P Books Publishing

10. Colors

color	**warna**	[varnə]
shade (tint)	**sisip warna**	[sisip varnə]
hue	**warna**	[varnə]
rainbow	**pelangi**	[pɛlaɲi]
white (adj)	**putih**	[putih]
black (adj)	**hitam**	[hitam]
gray (adj)	**abu-abu**	[abu abu]
green (adj)	**hijau**	[hidʒau]
yellow (adj)	**kuning**	[kuniŋ]
red (adj)	**merah**	[merah]
blue (adj)	**biru**	[biru]
light blue (adj)	**biru muda**	[biru mudə]
pink (adj)	**merah jambu**	[merah dʒambu]
orange (adj)	**oren, jingga**	[oren], [dʒiŋgə]
violet (adj)	**ungu**	[uŋu]
brown (adj)	**coklat**	[tʃoklat]
golden (adj)	**emas**	[ɛmas]
silvery (adj)	**keperak-perakan**	[kɛperak perakan]
beige (adj)	**kuning air**	[kuniŋ air]
cream (adj)	**putih kuning**	[putih kuniŋ]
turquoise (adj)	**firus**	[firus]
cherry red (adj)	**merah ceri**	[merah tʃeri]
lilac (adj)	**ungu**	[uŋu]
crimson (adj)	**merah lembayung**	[merah lɛmbajuŋ]
light (adj)	**terang**	[tɛraŋ]
dark (adj)	**gelap**	[glap]
bright, vivid (adj)	**berkilau**	[bɛrkilau]
colored (pencils)	**berwarna**	[bɛrvarnə]
color (e.g., ~ film)	**berwarna**	[bɛrvarnə]
black-and-white (adj)	**hitam-putih**	[hitam putih]
plain (one-colored)	**polos**	[polos]
multicolored (adj)	**beraneka warna**	[bɛraneka varnə]

11. Units of measurement

weight	**berat**	[brat]
length	**panjang**	[pandʒaŋ]

width	kelebaran	[kɛlebaran]
height	ketinggian	[kɛtiŋgian]
depth	kedalaman	[kɛdalaman]
volume	isi padu	[isi padu]
area	luas	[luas]

gram	gram	[gram]
milligram	miligram	[miligram]
kilogram	kilogram	[kilogram]
ton	tan	[tan]
pound	paun	[paun]
ounce	auns	[auns]

meter	meter	[metɛr]
millimeter	milimeter	[milimetɛr]
centimeter	sentimeter	[sentimetɛr]
kilometer	kilometer	[kilometɛr]
mile	batu	[batu]

inch	inci	[intʃi]
foot	kaki	[kaki]
yard	ela	[elə]

square meter	meter persegi	[metɛr pɛrsɛgi]
hectare	hektar	[hektar]
liter	liter	[litɛr]
degree	darjah	[dardʒah]
volt	volt	[volt]
ampere	ampere	[ampɛrɛ]
horsepower	kuasa kuda	[kuasa kudə]

quantity	kuantiti	[kuantiti]
a little bit of …	sedikit	[sɛdikit]
half	setengah	[sɛtɛŋah]
dozen	dozen	[dozen]
piece (item)	buah	[buah]

| size | saiz, ukuran | [sajz], [ukuran] |
| scale (map ~) | skala | [skalə] |

minimal (adj)	minimum	[minimum]
the smallest (adj)	terkecil	[tɛrkɛtʃil]
medium (adj)	sederhana	[sɛdɛrhanə]
maximal (adj)	maksimum	[maksimum]
the largest (adj)	terbesar	[tɛrbɛsar]

12. Containers

| canning jar (glass ~) | balang | [balaŋ] |
| can | tin | [tin] |

bucket	**baldi**	[baldi]
barrel	**tong**	[toŋ]
wash basin (e.g., plastic ~)	**besen**	[besen]
tank (100L water ~)	**tangki**	[taŋki]
hip flask	**kelalang, flask**	[kɛlalaŋ], [flas]
jerrycan	**tin**	[tin]
tank (e.g., tank car)	**tangki**	[taŋki]
mug	**koleh**	[koleh]
cup (of coffee, etc.)	**cawan**	[ʧavan]
saucer	**alas cawan**	[alas ʧavan]
glass (tumbler)	**gelas**	[glas]
wine glass	**gelas**	[glas]
stock pot (soup pot)	**periuk**	[priu]
bottle (~ of wine)	**botol**	[botol]
neck (of the bottle, etc.)	**leher**	[leher]
carafe (decanter)	**serahi**	[sɛrahi]
pitcher	**kendi**	[kɛndi]
vessel (container)	**bekas**	[bɛkas]
pot (crock, stoneware ~)	**belanga**	[bɛlaŋə]
vase	**vas**	[vas]
flacon, bottle (perfume ~)	**botol**	[botol]
vial, small bottle	**buli-buli**	[buli buli]
tube (of toothpaste)	**tiub**	[tiub]
sack (bag)	**karung**	[karuŋ]
bag (paper ~, plastic ~)	**peket**	[pekeʈ]
pack (of cigarettes, etc.)	**kotak**	[kota]
box (e.g., shoebox)	**kotak, peti**	[kotak], [pɛti]
crate	**kotak**	[kota]
basket	**bakul**	[bakul]

MAIN VERBS

T&P Books Publishing

to advise (vt)	menasihatkan	[mɛnasihatkan]
to agree (say yes)	setuju	[sɛtudʒu]
to answer (vi, vt)	menjawab	[mɛndʒavab]
to apologize (vi)	minta maaf	[minta maaf]
to arrive (vi)	datang	[dataŋ]
to ask (~ oneself)	menyoal	[mɛnjoal]
to ask (~ sb to do sth)	meminta	[mɛmintə]
to be (~ a teacher)	ialah	[ialah]
to be (~ on a diet)	sedang	[sɛdaŋ]
to be afraid	takut	[takut]
to be hungry	lapar	[lapar]
to be interested in …	menaruh minat	[mɛnaruh minat]
to be needed	diperlukan	[dipɛrlukan]
to be surprised	hairan	[hajran]
to be thirsty	haus	[haus]
to begin (vt)	memulakan	[mɛmulakan]
to belong to …	kepunyaan	[kɛpunjaan]
to boast (vi)	bercakap besar	[bɛrtʃakap bɛsar]
to break (split into pieces)	memecahkan	[mɛmɛtʃahkan]
to call (~ for help)	memanggil	[mɛmaŋgil]
can (v aux)	boleh	[bole]
to catch (vt)	menangkap	[mɛnaŋkap]
to change (vt)	mengubah	[mɛŋubah]
to choose (select)	memilih	[mɛmilih]
to come down (the stairs)	turun	[turun]
to compare (vt)	membandingkan	[mɛmbandiŋkan]
to complain (vi, vt)	mengadu	[mɛŋadu]
to confuse (mix up)	mengelirukan	[mɛŋɛlirukan]
to continue (vt)	meneruskan	[mɛnɛruskan]
to control (vt)	mengawal	[mɛŋaval]
to cook (dinner)	memasak	[mɛmasa]
to cost (vt)	berharga	[bɛrhargə]
to count (add up)	menghitung	[mɛŋɣitun]
to count on …	mengharapkan	[mɛŋɣarapkan]
to create (vt)	menciptakan	[mɛntʃiptakan]
to cry (weep)	menangis	[mɛnaŋis]

14. The most important verbs. Part 2

to deceive (vi, vt)	menipu	[mɛnipu]
to decorate (tree, street)	menghiasi	[mɛŋyiasi]
to defend (a country, etc.)	membela	[mɛmbɛlə]
to demand (request firmly)	menuntut	[mɛnuntut]
to dig (vt)	menggali	[mɛŋgali]
to discuss (vt)	membincangkan	[mɛmbintʃaŋkan]
to do (vt)	membuat	[mɛmbuat]
to doubt (have doubts)	ragu-ragu	[ragu ragu]
to drop (let fall)	tercicir	[tɛrtʃitʃir]
to enter (room, house, etc.)	masuk	[masu]
to excuse (forgive)	memaafkan	[mɛmaafkan]
to exist (vi)	wujud	[vudʒud]
to expect (foresee)	menjangkakan	[mɛndʒaŋkakan]
to explain (vt)	menjelaskan	[mɛndʒɛlaskan]
to fall (vi)	jatuh	[dʒatuh]
to find (vt)	menemui	[mɛnɛmui]
to finish (vt)	menamatkan	[mɛnamatkan]
to fly (vi)	terbang	[tɛrbaŋ]
to follow ... (come after)	mengikuti	[mɛŋikuti]
to forget (vi, vt)	melupakan	[mɛlupakan]
to forgive (vt)	memaafkan	[mɛmaafkan]
to give (vt)	memberi	[mɛmbri]
to give a hint	memberi bayangan	[mɛmbri bajaŋan]
to go (on foot)	berjalan	[bɛrdʒalan]
to go for a swim	mandi	[mandi]
to go out (for dinner, etc.)	keluar	[kɛluar]
to guess (the answer)	meneka	[mɛnɛkə]
to have (vt)	mempunyai	[mɛmpunjai]
to have breakfast	makan pagi	[makan pagi]
to have dinner	makan malam	[makan malam]
to have lunch	makan tengah hari	[makan tɛŋah hari]
to hear (vt)	mendengar	[mɛndɛŋar]
to help (vt)	membantu	[mɛmbantu]
to hide (vt)	menyorokkan	[mɛnjorokkan]
to hope (vi, vt)	harap	[harap]
to hunt (vi, vt)	memburu	[mɛmburu]
to hurry (vi)	tergesa-gesa	[tɛrgɛsa gɛsə]

15. The most important verbs. Part 3

to inform (vt)	**memberitahu**	[mɛmbritahu]
to insist (vi, vt)	**mendesak**	[mɛndɛsa]
to insult (vt)	**menghina**	[mɛŋɣinə]
to invite (vt)	**menjemput**	[mɛndʒɛmput]
to joke (vi)	**berjenaka**	[bɛrdʒɛnakə]
to keep (vt)	**menyimpan**	[mɛnjimpan]
to keep silent, to hush	**diam**	[diam]
to kill (vt)	**membunuh**	[mɛmbunuh]
to know (sb)	**kenal**	[kɛnal]
to know (sth)	**tahu**	[tahu]
to laugh (vi)	**ketawa**	[kɛtavə]
to liberate (city, etc.)	**membebaskan**	[mɛmbebaskan]
to like (I like …)	**suka**	[sukə]
to look for … (search)	**mencari**	[mɛntʃari]
to love (sb)	**mencintai**	[mɛntʃintai]
to make a mistake	**salah**	[salah]
to manage, to run	**memimpin**	[mɛmimpin]
to mean (signify)	**bererti**	[bɛrɛrti]
to mention (talk about)	**menyebut**	[mɛnjebut]
to miss (school, etc.)	**meninggalkan**	[mɛniŋgalkan]
to notice (see)	**memerhatikan**	[mɛmɛrhatikan]
to object (vi, vt)	**membantah**	[mɛmbantah]
to observe (see)	**menyaksikan**	[mɛnjaksikan]
to open (vt)	**membuka**	[mɛmbukə]
to order (meal, etc.)	**menempah**	[mɛnɛmpah]
to order (mil.)	**memerintah**	[mɛmɛrintah]
to own (possess)	**memiliki**	[mɛmiliki]
to participate (vi)	**menyertai**	[mɛnjertai]
to pay (vi, vt)	**membayar**	[mɛmbajar]
to permit (vt)	**mengizinkan**	[mɛŋiziŋkan]
to plan (vt)	**merancang**	[mɛrantʃaŋ]
to play (children)	**bermain**	[bɛrmajn]
to pray (vi, vt)	**bersembahyang**	[bɛrsɛmbahjaŋ]
to prefer (vt)	**lebih suka**	[lɛbih sukə]
to promise (vt)	**menjanji**	[mɛndʒandʒi]
to pronounce (vt)	**menyebut**	[mɛnjebut]
to propose (vt)	**mencadangkan**	[mɛntʃadaŋkan]
to punish (vt)	**menghukum**	[mɛŋɣukum]

16. The most important verbs. Part 4

to read (vi, vt)	**membaca**	[mɛmbatʃə]
to recommend (vt)	**menasihatkan**	[mɛnasihatkan]

to refuse (vi, vt)	menolak	[mɛnola]
to regret (be sorry)	terkilan	[tɛrkilan]
to rent (sth from sb)	menyewa	[mɛnjevə]
to repeat (say again)	mengulang	[mɛŋulaŋ]
to reserve, to book	menempah	[mɛnɛmpah]
to run (vi)	lari	[lari]
to save (rescue)	menyelamatkan	[mɛnjelamatkan]
to say (~ thank you)	berkata	[bɛrkatə]
to scold (vt)	memarahi	[mɛmarahi]
to see (vt)	melihat	[mɛlihat]
to sell (vt)	menjual	[mɛndʒual]
to send (vt)	mengirim	[mɛŋirim]
to shoot (vi)	menembak	[mɛnemba]
to shout (vi)	berteriak	[bɛrtɛria]
to show (vt)	menunjukkan	[mɛnundʒukkan]
to sign (document)	menandatangani	[mɛnandataŋani]
to sit down (vi)	duduk	[dudu]
to smile (vi)	senyum	[sɛnjum]
to speak (vi, vt)	bercakap	[bɛrtʃakap]
to steal (money, etc.)	mencuri	[mɛntʃuri]
to stop (for pause, etc.)	berhenti	[bɛrhɛnti]
to stop	memberhentikan	[mɛmbɛrhɛntikan]
(please ~ calling me)		
to study (vt)	mempelajari	[mɛmpɛladʒari]
to swim (vi)	berenang	[bɛrɛnaŋ]
to take (vt)	mengambil	[mɛŋambil]
to think (vi, vt)	berfikir	[bɛrfikir]
to threaten (vt)	mengugut	[mɛŋugut]
to touch (with hands)	menyentuh	[mɛnjentuh]
to translate (vt)	menterjemahkan	[mɛntɛrdʒemahkan]
to trust (vt)	mempercayai	[mɛmpɛrtʃajai]
to try (attempt)	mencuba	[mɛntʃubə]
to turn (e.g., ~ left)	membelok	[mɛmblo]
to underestimate (vt)	memperkecilkan	[mɛmpɛrkɛtʃilkan]
to understand (vt)	memahami	[mɛmahami]
to unite (vt)	menyatukan	[mɛnjatukan]
to wait (vt)	menunggu	[mɛnuŋgu]
to want (wish, desire)	mahu, hendak	[mahu], [hɛnda]
to warn (vt)	memperingati	[mɛmpɛriŋati]
to work (vi)	bekerja	[bɛkɛrdʒə]
to write (vt)	menulis	[mɛnulis]
to write down	mencatat	[mɛntʃatat]

TIME. CALENDAR

T&P Books Publishing

17. Weekdays

Monday	**Hari Isnin**	[hari isnin]
Tuesday	**Hari Selasa**	[hari sɛlasə]
Wednesday	**Hari Rabu**	[hari rabu]
Thursday	**Hari Khamis**	[hari kamis]
Friday	**Hari Jumaat**	[hari dʒumaat]
Saturday	**Hari Sabtu**	[hari sabtu]
Sunday	**Hari Ahad**	[hari ahad]
today (adv)	**hari ini**	[hari ini]
tomorrow (adv)	**besok**	[beso]
the day after tomorrow	**besok lusa**	[besok lusə]
yesterday (adv)	**semalam**	[sɛmalam]
the day before yesterday	**kelmarin**	[kɛlmarin]
day	**hari**	[hari]
working day	**hari kerja**	[hari kɛrdʒə]
public holiday	**cuti umum**	[ʧuti umum]
day off	**hari kelepasan**	[hari kɛlɛpasan]
weekend	**hujung minggu**	[hudʒuŋ miŋgu]
all day long	**seluruh hari**	[sɛluruh hari]
the next day (adv)	**pada hari berikutnya**	[pada hari bɛrikutnjə]
two days ago	**dua hari lepas**	[dua hari lɛpas]
the day before	**menjelang**	[mɛndʒɛlaŋ]
daily (adj)	**harian**	[harian]
every day (adv)	**setiap hari**	[sɛtiap hari]
week	**minggu**	[miŋgu]
last week (adv)	**pada minggu lepas**	[pada miŋgu lɛpas]
next week (adv)	**pada minggu berikutnya**	[pada miŋgu bɛrikutnjə]
weekly (adj)	**mingguan**	[miŋguan]
every week (adv)	**setiap minggu**	[sɛtiap miŋgu]
twice a week	**dua kali seminggu**	[dua kali sɛmiŋgu]
every Tuesday	**setiap Hari Selasa**	[sɛtiap hari sɛlasə]

18. Hours. Day and night

morning	**pagi**	[pagi]
in the morning	**pagi hari**	[pagi hari]
noon, midday	**tengah hari**	[tɛŋah hari]
in the afternoon	**petang hari**	[pɛtaŋ hari]
evening	**petang, malam**	[pɛtaŋ], [malam]

in the evening	pada waktu petang	[pada vaktu pɛtaŋ]
night	malam	[malam]
at night	pada malam	[pada malam]
midnight	tengah malam	[tɛŋah malam]

second	saat	[saat]
minute	minit	[minit]
hour	jam	[dʒam]
half an hour	separuh jam	[sɛparuh dʒam]
a quarter-hour	suku jam	[suku dʒam]
fifteen minutes	lima belas minit	[lima blas minit]
24 hours	siang malam	[siaŋ malam]

sunrise	matahari terbit	[matahari tɛrbit]
dawn	subuh	[subuh]
early morning	awal pagi	[aval pagi]
sunset	matahari terbenam	[matahari tɛrbɛnam]

early in the morning	pagi-pagi	[pagi pagi]
this morning	pagi ini	[pagi ini]
tomorrow morning	besok pagi	[bɛsok pagi]

this afternoon	petang ini	[pɛtaŋ ini]
in the afternoon	petang hari	[pɛtaŋ hari]
tomorrow afternoon	besok petang	[besok pɛtaŋ]

tonight (this evening)	petang ini	[pɛtaŋ ini]
tomorrow night	besok malam	[besok malam]

at 3 o'clock sharp	pukul 3 tepat	[pukul tiga tɛpat]
about 4 o'clock	sekitar pukul 4	[sɛkitar pukul ɛmpat]
by 12 o'clock	sampai pukul 12	[sampaj pukul dua blas]

in 20 minutes	selepas 20 minit	[sɛlɛpas dua puluh minit]
in an hour	selepas satu jam	[sɛlɛpas satu dʒam]
on time (adv)	tepat pada masanya	[tɛpat pada masanjə]

a quarter to ...	kurang suku	[kuraŋ suku]
within an hour	selama sejam	[sɛlama sɛdʒam]
every 15 minutes	setiap 15 minit	[sɛtiap lima blas minit]
round the clock	siang malam	[siaŋ malam]

19. Months. Seasons

January	Januari	[dʒanuari]
February	Februari	[februari]
March	Mac	[matʃ]
April	April	[april]
May	Mei	[mej]
June	Jun	[dʒun]

July	**Julai**	[dʒulaj]
August	**Ogos**	[ogos]
September	**September**	[septembɛr]
October	**Oktober**	[oktobɛr]
November	**November**	[novembɛr]
December	**Disember**	[disembɛr]

spring	**musim bunga**	[musim buŋə]
in spring	**pada musim bunga**	[pada musim buŋə]
spring (as adj)	**musim bunga**	[musim buŋə]

summer	**musim panas**	[musim panas]
in summer	**pada musim panas**	[pada musim panas]
summer (as adj)	**musim panas**	[musim panas]

fall	**musim gugur**	[musim gugur]
in fall	**pada musim gugur**	[pada musim gugur]
fall (as adj)	**musim gugur**	[musim gugur]

winter	**musim sejuk**	[musim sɛdʒu]
in winter	**pada musim sejuk**	[pada musim sɛdʒu]
winter (as adj)	**musim sejuk**	[musim sɛdʒu]

month	**bulan**	[bulan]
this month	**pada bulan ini**	[pada bulan ini]
next month	**pada bulan berikutnya**	[pada bulan bɛrikutnjə]
last month	**pada bulan yang lepas**	[pada bulan jaŋ lɛpas]

a month ago	**sebulan lepas**	[sɛbulan lɛpas]
in a month (a month later)	**selepas satu bulan**	[sɛlɛpas satu bulan]
in 2 months (2 months later)	**selepas 2 bulan**	[sɛlɛpas dua bulan]
the whole month	**seluruh bulan**	[sɛluruh bulan]
all month long	**seluruh bulan**	[sɛluruh bulan]

monthly (~ magazine)	**bulanan**	[bulanan]
monthly (adv)	**setiap bulan**	[sɛtiap bulan]
every month	**setiap bulan**	[sɛtiap bulan]
twice a month	**dua kali sebulan**	[dua kali sɛbulan]

year	**tahun**	[tahun]
this year	**pada tahun ini**	[pada tahun ini]
next year	**pada tahun berikutnya**	[pada tahun bɛrikutnjə]
last year	**pada tahun yang lepas**	[pada tahun jaŋ lɛpas]

a year ago	**setahun lepas**	[setahun lɛpas]
in a year	**selepas satu tahun**	[sɛlɛpas satu tahun]
in two years	**selepas 2 tahun**	[sɛlɛpas dua tahun]
the whole year	**seluruh tahun**	[sɛluruh tahun]
all year long	**seluruh tahun**	[sɛluruh tahun]
every year	**setiap tahun**	[sɛtiap tahun]
annual (adj)	**tahunan**	[tahunan]

annually (adv)	**setiap tahun**	[sɛtiap tahun]
4 times a year	**empat kali setahun**	[ɛmpat kali sɛtahun]
date (e.g., today's ~)	**tarikh**	[tarih]
date (e.g., ~ of birth)	**tarikh**	[tarih]
calendar	**takwim**	[takvim]
half a year	**separuh tahun**	[sɛparuh tahun]
six months	**separuh tahun**	[sɛparuh tahun]
season (summer, etc.)	**musim**	[musim]
century	**abad**	[abad]

TRAVEL. HOTEL

T&P Books Publishing

20. Trip. Travel

tourism, travel	**pelancongan**	[pɛlanʧoŋan]
tourist	**pelancong**	[pɛlanʧoŋ]
trip, voyage	**pengembaraan**	[pɛŋɛmbaraan]
adventure	**petualangan**	[pɛtualaŋan]
trip, journey	**lawatan**	[lavatan]
vacation	**cuti**	[ʧuti]
to be on vacation	**bercuti**	[bɛrʧuti]
rest	**rehat**	[rehat]
train	**kereta api**	[kreta api]
by train	**naik kereta api**	[naik kreta api]
airplane	**kapal terbang**	[kapal tɛrbaŋ]
by airplane	**naik kapal terbang**	[naik kapal tɛrbaŋ]
by car	**naik kereta**	[naik kretə]
by ship	**naik kapal**	[naik kapal]
luggage	**bagasi**	[bagasi]
suitcase	**beg pakaian**	[beg pakajan]
luggage cart	**troli bagasi**	[troli bagasi]
passport	**pasport**	[pasport]
visa	**visa**	[visə]
ticket	**tiket**	[tiket]
air ticket	**tiket kapal terbang**	[tiket kapal tɛrbaŋ]
guidebook	**buku panduan pelancongan**	[buku panduan pɛlanʧoŋan]
map (tourist ~)	**peta**	[pɛtə]
area (rural ~)	**kawasan**	[kavasan]
place, site	**tempat duduk**	[tɛmpat dudu]
exotica (n)	**keeksotikan**	[kɛeksotikan]
exotic (adj)	**eksotik**	[eksoti]
amazing (adj)	**menakjubkan**	[mɛnakdʒubkan]
group	**kumpulan**	[kumpulan]
excursion, sightseeing tour	**darmawisata**	[darmavisatə]
guide (person)	**pemandu pelancong**	[pɛmandu pɛlanʧoŋ]

21. Hotel

hotel	**hotel**	[hotel]
motel	**motel**	[motel]

three-star (~ hotel)	tiga bintang	[tiga bintaŋ]
five-star	lima bintang	[lima bintaŋ]
to stay (in a hotel, etc.)	menumpang	[mɛnumpaŋ]

room	bilik	[bili]
single room	bilik untuk satu orang	[bilik untuk satu oraŋ]
double room	bilik kelamin	[bilik kɛlamin]
to book a room	menempah bilik	[mɛnempah bili]

| half board | penginapan tanpa makanan | [pɛɲinapan tanpa makanan] |
| full board | penginapan dengan makanan | [pɛɲinapan dɛŋan makanan] |

with bath	dengan tab mandi	[dɛŋan tab mandi]
with shower	dengan pancaran air	[dɛŋan pantʃaran air]
satellite television	televisyen satelit	[televiʃɛn satɛlit]
air-conditioner	penghawa dingin	[pɛŋɣava diɲin]
towel	tuala	[tualə]
key	kunci	[kuntʃi]

administrator	pentadbir	[pɛntadbir]
chambermaid	pengemas rumah	[pɛŋɛmas rumah]
porter, bellboy	porter	[portɛr]
doorman	penjaga pintu	[pɛndʒaga pintu]

restaurant	restoran	[restoran]
pub, bar	bar	[bar]
breakfast	makan pagi	[makan pagi]
dinner	makan malam	[makan malam]
buffet	jamuan berselerak	[dʒamuan bɛrsɛlera]

| lobby | ruang legar | [ruaŋ legar] |
| elevator | lif | [lif] |

| DO NOT DISTURB | JANGAN MENGGANGGU | [dʒaŋan mɛŋgaŋgu] |
| NO SMOKING | DILARANG MEROKOK! | [dilaraŋ mɛrokok] |

22. Sightseeing

monument	tugu	[tugu]
fortress	kubu	[kubu]
palace	istana	[istanə]
castle	istana kota	[istana kotə]
tower	menara	[mɛnarə]
mausoleum	mausoleum	[mausoleum]

| architecture | seni bina | [sɛni binə] |
| medieval (adj) | abad pertengahan | [abad pɛrtɛŋahan] |

ancient (adj)	**kuno**	[kuno]
national (adj)	**nasional**	[nasional]
famous (monument, etc.)	**terkenal**	[tɛrkɛnal]
tourist	**pelancong**	[pɛlantʃoŋ]
guide (person)	**pemandu**	[pɛmandu]
excursion, sightseeing tour	**darmawisata**	[darmavisatə]
to show (vt)	**menunjukkan**	[mɛnundʒukkan]
to tell (vt)	**menceritakan**	[mɛntʃɛritakan]
to find (vt)	**mendapati**	[mɛndapati]
to get lost (lose one's way)	**kehilangan**	[kɛhilaŋan]
map (e.g., subway ~)	**peta**	[pɛtə]
map (e.g., city ~)	**pelan**	[plan]
souvenir, gift	**cenderamata**	[tʃɛndramatə]
gift shop	**kedai cenderamata**	[kedaj tʃɛndramatə]
to take pictures	**mengambil gambar**	[mɛŋambil gambar]
to have one's picture taken	**bergambar**	[bɛrgambar]

TRANSPORTATION

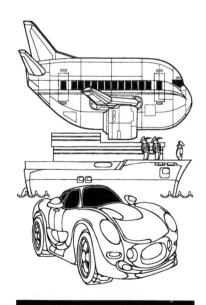

T&P Books Publishing

airport	**lapangan terbang**	[lapaŋan tɛrbaŋ]
airplane	**kapal terbang**	[kapal tɛrbaŋ]
airline	**syarikat penerbangan**	[ɕarikat pɛnɛrbaŋan]
air traffic controller	**pengawal lalu lintas udara**	[pɛŋaval lalu lintas udarə]
departure	**berlepas**	[bɛrlɛpas]
arrival	**ketibaan**	[kɛtibaan]
to arrive (by plane)	**tiba**	[tibə]
departure time	**waktu berlepas**	[vaktu bɛrlɛpas]
arrival time	**waktu ketibaan**	[vaktu kɛtibaan]
to be delayed	**terlewat**	[tɛrlevat]
flight delay	**kelewatan penerbangan**	[kelevatan pɛnɛrbaŋan]
information board	**skrin paparan maklumat**	[skrin paparan maklumat]
information	**maklumat**	[maklumat]
to announce (vt)	**mengumumkan**	[mɛŋumumkan]
flight (e.g., next ~)	**penerbangan**	[pɛnɛrbaŋan]
customs	**kastam**	[kastam]
customs officer	**anggota kastam**	[aŋgota kastam]
customs declaration	**ikrar kastam**	[ikrar kastam]
to fill out (vt)	**mengisi**	[mɛŋisi]
to fill out the declaration	**mengisi ikrar kastam**	[mɛŋisi ikrar kastam]
passport control	**pemeriksaan pasport**	[pɛmɛriksaan pasport]
luggage	**bagasi**	[bagasi]
hand luggage	**bagasi tangan**	[bagasi taŋan]
luggage cart	**troli**	[troli]
landing	**pendaratan**	[pɛndaratan]
landing strip	**jalur mendarat**	[dʒalur mɛndarat]
to land (vi)	**mendarat**	[mɛndarat]
airstair (passenger stair)	**tangga kapal terbang**	[taŋga kapal tɛrbaŋ]
check-in	**pendaftaran**	[pɛndaftaran]
check-in counter	**kaunter daftar masuk**	[kauntɛr daftar masu]
to check-in (vi)	**berdaftar**	[bɛrdaftar]
boarding pass	**pas masuk**	[pas masu]
departure gate	**pintu berlepas**	[pintu bɛrlɛpas]
transit	**transit**	[transit]

to wait (vt)	menunggu	[mɛnuŋgu]
departure lounge	balai menunggu	[balaj mɛnuŋgu]
to see off	menghantarkan	[mɛɲantarkan]
to say goodbye	minta diri	[minta diri]

24. Airplane

airplane	kapal terbang	[kapal tɛrbaŋ]
air ticket	tiket kapal terbang	[tiket kapal tɛrbaŋ]
airline	syarikat penerbangan	[ɕarikat pɛnɛrbaŋan]
airport	lapangan terbang	[lapaŋan tɛrbaŋ]
supersonic (adj)	supersonik	[supersoni]

captain	kapten kapal	[kaptɛn kapal]
crew	anak buah	[anak buah]
pilot	juruterbang	[dʒurutɛrbaŋ]
flight attendant (fem.)	pramugari	[pramugari]
navigator	pemandu	[pɛmandu]

wings	sayap	[sajap]
tail	ekor	[ekor]
cockpit	kokpit	[kokpit]
engine	enjin	[endʒin]
undercarriage (landing gear)	roda pendarat	[roda pɛndarat]
turbine	turbin	[turbin]

propeller	baling-baling	[baliŋ baliŋ]
black box	kotak hitam	[kotak hitam]
yoke (control column)	kemudi	[kɛmudi]
fuel	bahan bakar	[bahan bakar]

safety card	kad keselamatan	[kad kɛsɛlamatan]
oxygen mask	topeng oksigen	[topeŋ oksigɛn]
uniform	pakaian seragam	[pakajan sɛragam]
life vest	jaket keselamatan	[dʒaket kɛsɛlamatan]
parachute	payung terjun	[pajuŋ tɛrdʒun]

takeoff	berlepas	[bɛrlɛpas]
to take off (vi)	berlepas	[bɛrlɛpas]
runway	landasan berlepas	[landasan bɛrlɛpas]

visibility	darjah penglihatan	[dardʒah pɛŋlihatan]
flight (act of flying)	penerbangan	[pɛnɛrbaŋan]
altitude	ketinggian	[kɛtiŋgian]
air pocket	lubang udara	[lubaŋ udarə]

seat	tempat duduk	[tɛmpat dudu]
headphones	pendengar telinga	[pɛndɛŋar tɛliŋə]
folding tray (tray table)	meja lipat	[medʒa lipat]

| airplane window | tingkap kapal terbang | [tiŋkap kapal tɛrbaŋ] |
| aisle | laluan | [laluan] |

25. Train

train	kereta api	[kreta api]
commuter train	tren elektrik	[tren elektri]
express train	kereta api cepat	[kreta api tʃɛpat]
diesel locomotive	lokomotif	[lokomotif]
steam locomotive	kereta api	[kreta api]

| passenger car | gerabak penumpang | [gɛrabak pɛnumpaŋ] |
| dining car | gerabak makan minum | [gɛrabak makan minum] |

rails	rel	[rel]
railroad	jalan kereta api	[dʒalan kreta api]
railway tie	kayu landas	[kaju landas]

platform (railway ~)	platform	[platform]
track (~ 1, 2, etc.)	trek landasan	[trek landasan]
semaphore	lampu isyarat	[lampu iɕarat]
station	stesen	[stesen]

engineer (train driver)	pemandu kereta api	[pɛmandu kreta api]
porter (of luggage)	porter	[portɛr]
car attendant	konduktor kereta api	[konduktor kreta api]
passenger	penumpang	[pɛnumpaŋ]
conductor	konduktor	[konduktor]
(ticket inspector)		

| corridor (in train) | koridor | [koridor] |
| emergency brake | brek kecemasan | [brek kɛtʃɛmasan] |

compartment	petak gerabak	[petak gɛraba]
berth	bangku	[baŋku]
upper berth	bangku atas	[baŋku atas]
lower berth	bangku bawah	[baŋku bavah]
bed linen, bedding	linen	[linen]

ticket	tiket	[tiket]
schedule	jadual waktu	[dʒadual vaktu]
information display	paparan jadual	[paparan dʒadual]

to leave, to depart	berlepas	[bɛrlɛpas]
departure (of train)	perlepasan	[pɛrlɛpasan]
to arrive (ab. train)	tiba	[tibə]
arrival	ketibaan	[kɛtibaan]

| to arrive by train | datang naik kereta api | [dataŋ naik kreta api] |
| to get on the train | naik kereta api | [naik kreta api] |

to get off the train	turun kereta api	[turun kreta api]
train wreck	kemalangan	[kɛmalaŋan]
to derail (vi)	keluar rel	[kɛluar rel]

steam locomotive	kereta api	[kreta api]
stoker, fireman	tukang api	[tukaŋ api]
firebox	tungku	[tuŋku]
coal	arang	[araŋ]

26. Ship

| ship | kapal | [kapal] |
| vessel | kapal | [kapal] |

steamship	kapal api	[kapal api]
riverboat	kapal	[kapal]
cruise ship	kapal laut	[kapal laut]
cruiser	kapal penjelajah	[kapal pɛndʒɛladʒah]

yacht	kapal persiaran	[kapal pɛrsiaran]
tugboat	kapal tunda	[kapal tundə]
barge	tongkang	[toŋkaŋ]
ferry	feri	[feri]

| sailing ship | kapal layar | [kapal lajar] |
| brigantine | kapal brigantine | [kapal brigantinɛ] |

| ice breaker | kapal pemecah ais | [kapal pɛmɛtʃah ajs] |
| submarine | kapal selam | [kapal sɛlam] |

boat (flat-bottomed ~)	perahu	[prahu]
dinghy (lifeboat)	sekoci	[sɛkotʃi]
lifeboat	sekoci penyelamat	[sɛkotʃi pɛnjelamat]
motorboat	motobot	[motobot]

captain	kapten	[kaptɛn]
seaman	kelasi	[kɛlasi]
sailor	pelaut	[pɛlaut]
crew	anak buah	[anak buah]

boatswain	nakhoda	[naχodə]
ship's boy	kadet kapal	[kadet kapal]
cook	tukang masak	[tukaŋ masa]
ship's doctor	doktor kapal	[doktor kapal]

deck	dek	[de]
mast	tiang	[tiaŋ]
sail	layar	[lajar]
hold	palka	[palkə]
bow (prow)	haluan	[haluan]

stern	buritan	[buritan]
oar	kayuh	[kajuh]
screw propeller	baling-baling	[baliŋ baliŋ]

cabin	kabin, bilik	[kabin], [bili]
wardroom	bilik pegawai kapal	[bilik pɛgavaj kapal]
engine room	bilik enjin	[bilik endʒin]
bridge	anjungan kapal	[andʒuŋan kapal]
radio room	bilik siaran radio	[bilik siaran radio]
wave (radio)	gelombang	[gɛlombaŋ]
logbook	buku log	[buku log]

spyglass	teropong kecil	[tɛropoŋ kɛtʃil]
bell	loceng	[lotʃeŋ]
flag	bendera	[bɛnderə]

| hawser (mooring ~) | tali | [tali] |
| knot (bowline, etc.) | simpul | [simpul] |

| deckrails | susur tangan | [susur taŋan] |
| gangway | tangga kapal | [taŋga kapal] |

anchor	sauh	[sauh]
to weigh anchor	mengangkat sauh	[mɛŋaŋkat sauh]
to drop anchor	berlabuh	[bɛrlabuh]
anchor chain	rantai sauh	[rantaj sauh]

port (harbor)	pelabuhan	[pɛlabuhan]
quay, wharf	jeti	[dʒeti]
to berth (moor)	merapat	[mɛrapat]
to cast off	berlepas	[bɛrlɛpas]

trip, voyage	pengembaraan	[pɛŋɛmbaraan]
cruise (sea trip)	pelayaran pesiaran	[pɛlajaran pɛsiaran]
course (route)	haluan	[haluan]
route (itinerary)	laluan	[laluan]

fairway (safe water channel)	aluran pelayaran	[aluran pɛlajaran]
shallows	beting	[bɛtiŋ]
to run aground	karam	[karam]

storm	badai	[badaj]
signal	peluit	[pɛluit]
to sink (vi)	tenggelam	[tɛŋgɛlam]
Man overboard!	Orang jatuh ke laut!	[oraŋ dʒatuh kɛ laut]
SOS (distress signal)	SOS	[sos]
ring buoy	pelambung keselamatan	[pɛlambuŋ kɛsɛlamatan]

CITY

T&P Books Publishing

bus	**bas**	[bas]
streetcar	**trem**	[trem]
trolley bus	**bas elektrik**	[bas elektri]
route (of bus, etc.)	**laluan**	[laluan]
number (e.g., bus ~)	**nombor**	[nombor]
to go by …	**naik**	[nai]
to get on (~ the bus)	**naik**	[nai]
to get off …	**turun**	[turun]
stop (e.g., bus ~)	**perhentian**	[pɛrhɛntian]
next stop	**perhentian berikut**	[pɛrhɛntian bɛrikut]
terminus	**perhentian akhir**	[pɛrhɛntian aχir]
schedule	**jadual waktu**	[dʒadual vaktu]
to wait (vt)	**menunggu**	[mɛnuŋgu]
ticket	**tiket**	[tiket]
fare	**harga tiket**	[harga tiket]
cashier (ticket seller)	**juruwang, kasyier**	[dʒuruvaŋ], [kaʃier]
ticket inspection	**pemeriksaan tiket**	[pɛmɛriksaan tiket]
ticket inspector	**konduktor**	[konduktor]
to be late (for …)	**lambat**	[lambat]
to miss (~ the train, etc.)	**ketinggalan**	[kɛtiŋgalan]
to be in a hurry	**tergesa-gesa**	[tɛrgɛsa gɛsə]
taxi, cab	**teksi**	[teksi]
taxi driver	**pemandu teksi**	[pɛmandu teksi]
by taxi	**naik teksi**	[naik tɛksi]
taxi stand	**perhentian teksi**	[pɛrhɛntian teksi]
to call a taxi	**memanggil teksi**	[mɛmaŋgil teksi]
to take a taxi	**mengambil teksi**	[mɛŋambil teksi]
traffic	**lalu lintas, trafik**	[lalu lintas], [trafi]
traffic jam	**kesesakan trafik**	[kɛsɛsakan trafi]
rush hour	**jam sibuk**	[dʒam sibu]
to park (vi)	**meletak kereta**	[mɛlɛtak kretə]
to park (vt)	**meletak**	[mɛlɛta]
parking lot	**tempat meletak**	[tɛmpat mɛlɛta]
subway	**LRT**	[ɛl ar ti]
station	**stesen**	[stesen]
to take the subway	**naik LRT**	[naik ɛl ar ti]

| train | kereta api, tren | [kreta api], [tren] |
| train station | stesen kereta api | [stesen kreta api] |

28. City. Life in the city

city, town	bandar	[bandar]
capital city	ibu negara	[ibu nɛgarə]
village	kampung	[kampuŋ]

city map	pelan bandar	[plan bandar]
downtown	pusat bandar	[pusat bandar]
suburb	pinggir bandar	[piŋgir bandar]
suburban (adj)	pinggir bandar	[piŋgir bandar]

outskirts	pinggir	[piŋgir]
environs (suburbs)	persekitaran	[pɛrɛekitaran]
city block	blok	[blo]
residential block (area)	blok kediaman	[blok kɛdiaman]

traffic	lalu lintas, trafik	[lalu lintas], [trafi]
traffic lights	lampu isyarat	[lampu iɕarat]
public transportation	pengangkutan awam bandar	[pɛŋaŋkutan avam bandar]
intersection	persimpangan	[pɛrsimpaŋan]

crosswalk	lintasan pejalan kaki	[lintasan pɛdʒalan kaki]
pedestrian underpass	terowong pejalan kaki	[tɛrovoŋ pɛdʒalan kaki]
to cross (~ the street)	melintas	[mɛlintas]
pedestrian	pejalan kaki	[pɛdʒalan kaki]
sidewalk	kaki lima	[kaki limə]

bridge	jambatan	[dʒambatan]
embankment (river walk)	jalan tepi sungai	[dʒalan tɛpi suŋaj]
fountain	pancutan air	[panʧutan air]

allée (garden walkway)	lorong	[loroŋ]
park	taman	[taman]
boulevard	boulevard	[bulevard]
square	dataran	[dataran]
avenue (wide street)	lebuh	[lɛbuh]
street	jalan	[dʒalan]
side street	lorong	[loroŋ]
dead end	buntu	[buntu]

house	rumah	[rumah]
building	bangunan	[baŋunan]
skyscraper	cakar langit	[ʧakar laŋit]

| facade | muka | [mukə] |
| roof | bumbung | [bumbuŋ] |

window	**tingkap**	[tiŋkap]
arch	**lengkung**	[lɛŋkuŋ]
column	**tiang**	[tiaŋ]
corner	**sudut**	[sudut]

store window	**cermin pameran**	[tʃɛrmin pameran]
signboard (store sign, etc.)	**papan nama**	[papan namə]
poster (e.g., playbill)	**poster**	[postɛr]
advertising poster	**poster iklan**	[postɛr iklan]
billboard	**papan iklan**	[papan iklan]

garbage, trash	**sampah**	[sampah]
trash can (public ~)	**tong sampah**	[toŋ sampah]
to litter (vi)	**menyepah**	[mɛnjepah]
garbage dump	**tempat sampah**	[tɛmpat sampah]

phone booth	**pondok telefon**	[pondok telefon]
lamppost	**tiang lampu jalan**	[tiaŋ lampu dʒalan]
bench (park ~)	**bangku**	[baŋku]

police officer	**anggota polis**	[aŋgota polis]
police	**polis**	[polis]
beggar	**pengemis**	[pɛŋɛmis]
homeless (n)	**orang yang tiada tempat berteduh**	[oraŋ jaŋ tiada tɛmpat bɛrtɛduh]

29. Urban institutions

store	**kedai**	[kɛdaj]
drugstore, pharmacy	**kedai ubat**	[kɛdaj ubat]
eyeglass store	**kedai optik**	[kɛdaj opti]
shopping mall	**pusat membeli-belah**	[pusat membli blah]
supermarket	**pasaraya**	[pasarajə]

bakery	**kedai roti**	[kɛdaj roti]
baker	**pembakar roti**	[pɛmbakar roti]
pastry shop	**kedai kuih**	[kɛdaj kuih]
grocery store	**barang-barang runcit**	[baraŋ baraŋ runtʃit]
butcher shop	**kedai daging**	[kɛdaj dagiŋ]

| produce store | **kedai sayur** | [kɛdaj sajur] |
| market | **pasar** | [pasar] |

coffee house	**kedai kopi**	[kɛdaj kopi]
restaurant	**restoran**	[restoran]
pub, bar	**kedai bir**	[kɛdaj bir]
pizzeria	**kedai piza**	[kɛdaj pizə]

| hair salon | **kedai gunting rambut** | [kɛdaj guntiŋ rambut] |
| post office | **pejabat pos** | [pɛdʒabat pos] |

| dry cleaners | kedai cucian kering | [kɛdaj ʧuʧian kɛriŋ] |
| photo studio | studio foto | [studio foto] |

shoe store	kedai kasut	[kɛdaj kasut]
bookstore	kedai buku	[kɛdaj buku]
sporting goods store	kedai barang sukan	[kɛdaj baraŋ sukan]

clothes repair shop	pembaikan baju	[pɛmbaikan badʒu]
formal wear rental	sewaan kostum	[sevaan kostum]
video rental store	sewa filem	[seva filɛm]

circus	sarkas	[sarkas]
zoo	zoo	[zu]
movie theater	pawagam	[pavagam]
museum	muzium	[muzium]
library	perpustakaan	[pɛrpustakaan]

| theater | teater | [teatɛr] |
| opera (opera house) | opera | [opɛrə] |

| nightclub | kelab malam | [klab malam] |
| casino | kasino | [kasino] |

mosque	masjid	[masdʒid]
synagogue	saumaah	[saumaah]
cathedral	katedral	[katɛdral]

| temple | rumah ibadat | [rumah ibadat] |
| church | gereja | [gɛredʒə] |

college	institut	[institut]
university	universiti	[univɛrsiti]
school	sekolah	[sɛkolah]

| prefecture | prefekture | [prefekturɛ] |
| city hall | dewan bandaran | [devan bandaran] |

| hotel | hotel | [hotel] |
| bank | bank | [baŋ] |

| embassy | kedutaan besar | [kɛdutaan bɛsar] |
| travel agency | agensi pelancongan | [agensi pɛlanʧoŋan] |

| information office | pejabat penerangan | [pɛdʒabat pɛnɛraŋan] |
| currency exchange | pusat pertukaran mata wang | [pusat pɛrtukaran mata vaŋ] |

| subway | LRT | [ɛl ar ti] |
| hospital | hospital | [hospital] |

| gas station | stesen minyak | [stesen minja] |
| parking lot | tempat letak kereta | [tɛmpat lɛtak kretə] |

30. Signs

signboard (store sign, etc.)	papan nama	[papan namə]
notice (door sign, etc.)	tulisan	[tulisan]
poster	poster	[postɛr]
direction sign	penunjuk	[pɛnundʒu]
arrow (sign)	anak panah	[anak panah]

caution	peringatan	[pɛriŋatan]
warning sign	amaran	[amaran]
to warn (vt)	memperingati	[mɛmpɛriŋati]

rest day (weekly ~)	hari kelepasan	[hari kɛlɛpasan]
timetable (schedule)	jadual waktu	[dʒadual vaktu]
opening hours	waktu pejabat	[vaktu pɛdʒabat]

WELCOME!	SELAMAT DATANG!	[sɛlamat dataŋ]
ENTRANCE	MASUK	[masu]
EXIT	KELUAR	[kɛluar]

PUSH	TOLAK	[tola]
PULL	TARIK	[tari]
OPEN	BUKA	[bukə]
CLOSED	TUTUP	[tutup]

| WOMEN | PEREMPUAN | [pɛrɛmpuan] |
| MEN | LELAKI | [lɛlaki] |

DISCOUNTS	POTONGAN	[potoŋan]
SALE	JUALAN MURAH	[dʒualan murah]
NEW!	BARU!	[baru]
FREE	PERCUMA	[pɛrtʃumə]

ATTENTION!	PERHATIAN!	[pɛrhatian]
NO VACANCIES	TIDAK ADA TEMPAT DUDUK YANG KOSONG	[tidak ada tɛmpat duduk jaŋ kosoŋ]
RESERVED	DITEMPAH	[ditɛmpah]

| ADMINISTRATION | PENTADBIRAN | [pɛntadbiran] |
| STAFF ONLY | KAKITANGAN SAJA | [kakitaŋan sadʒə] |

BEWARE OF THE DOG!	AWAS, ANJING GANAS!	[avas], [andʒiŋ ganas]
NO SMOKING	DILARANG MEROKOK!	[dilaraŋ mɛrokok]
DO NOT TOUCH!	JANGAN SENTUH!	[dʒaŋan sɛntuh]

DANGEROUS	BERBAHAYA	[bɛrbahajə]
DANGER	BAHAYA	[bahajə]
HIGH VOLTAGE	VOLTAN TINGGI	[voltan tiŋgi]
NO SWIMMING!	DILARANG BERENANG!	[dilaraŋ bɛrɛnaŋ]
OUT OF ORDER	ROSAK	[rosa]
FLAMMABLE	MUDAH TERBAKAR	[mudah tɛrbakar]

FORBIDDEN	**DILARANG**	[dilaraŋ]
NO TRESPASSING!	**DILARANG MASUK!**	[dilaraŋ masuk]
WET PAINT	**CAT BASAH**	[tʃat basah]

31. Shopping

to buy (purchase)	**membeli**	[mɛmbli]
purchase	**belian**	[blian]
to go shopping	**membeli-belah**	[mɛmbli blah]
shopping	**berbelanja**	[bɛrblandʒə]

| to be open (ab. store) | **buka** | [bukə] |
| to be closed | **tutup** | [tutup] |

footwear, shoes	**kasut**	[kasut]
clothes, clothing	**pakaian**	[pakajan]
cosmetics	**alat solek**	[alat sole]
food products	**bahan makanan**	[bahan makanan]
gift, present	**hadiah**	[hadiah]

| salesman | **penjual** | [pɛndʒual] |
| saleswoman | **jurujual perempuan** | [dʒurudʒual pɛrɛmpuan] |

check out, cash desk	**tempat juruwang**	[tɛmpat dʒuruvaŋ]
mirror	**cermin**	[tʃɛrmin]
counter (store ~)	**kaunter**	[kaunter]
fitting room	**bilik acu**	[bilik atʃu]

to try on	**mencuba**	[mɛntʃubə]
to fit (ab. dress, etc.)	**sesuai**	[sɛsuaj]
to like (I like ...)	**suka**	[sukə]

price	**harga**	[hargə]
price tag	**tanda harga**	[tanda hargə]
to cost (vt)	**berharga**	[bɛrhargə]
How much?	**Berapa?**	[brapə]
discount	**potongan**	[potoŋan]

inexpensive (adj)	**tidak mahal**	[tidak mahal]
cheap (adj)	**murah**	[murah]
expensive (adj)	**mahal**	[mahal]
It's expensive	**Ini mahal**	[ini mahal]

rental (n)	**sewaan**	[sevaan]
to rent (~ a tuxedo)	**menyewa**	[mɛnjevə]
credit (trade credit)	**pinjaman**	[pindʒaman]
on credit (adv)	**dengan pinjaman**	[dɛŋan pindʒaman
	sewa beli	seva eli]

CLOTHING & ACCESSORIES

T&P Books Publishing

32. Outerwear. Coats

clothes	**pakaian**	[pakajan]
outerwear	**pakaian luar**	[pakajan luar]
winter clothing	**pakaian musim sejuk**	[pakajan musim sɛdʒu]
coat (overcoat)	**kot luaran**	[kot luaran]
fur coat	**kot bulu**	[kot bulu]
fur jacket	**jaket berbulu**	[dʒaket berbulu]
down coat	**kot bulu pelepah**	[kot bulu pɛlɛpah]
jacket (e.g., leather ~)	**jaket**	[dʒaket]
raincoat (trenchcoat, etc.)	**baju hujan**	[badʒu hudʒan]
waterproof (adj)	**kalis air**	[kalis air]

33. Men's & women's clothing

shirt (button shirt)	**baju**	[badʒu]
pants	**seluar**	[sɛluar]
jeans	**seluar jean**	[sɛluar dʒin]
suit jacket	**jaket**	[dʒaket]
suit	**suit**	[suit]
dress (frock)	**gaun**	[gaun]
skirt	**skirt**	[skirt]
blouse	**blaus**	[blaus]
knitted jacket (cardigan, etc.)	**jaket kait**	[dʒaket kait]
jacket (of woman's suit)	**jaket**	[dʒaket]
T-shirt	**baju kaus**	[badʒu kaus]
shorts (short trousers)	**seluar pendek**	[sɛluar pende]
tracksuit	**pakaian sukan**	[pakajan sukan]
bathrobe	**jubah mandi**	[dʒubah mandi]
pajamas	**pijama**	[pidʒamə]
sweater	**sweater**	[svetɛr]
pullover	**pullover**	[pullovɛr]
vest	**rompi**	[rompi]
tailcoat	**kot bajang**	[kot badʒaŋ]
tuxedo	**toksedo**	[toksedo]
uniform	**pakaian seragam**	[pakajan sɛragam]
workwear	**pakaian kerja**	[pakajan kɛrdʒə]

| overalls | baju monyet | [badʒu monjet] |
| coat (e.g., doctor's smock) | baju | [badʒu] |

34. Clothing. Underwear

underwear	pakaian dalam	[pakajan dalam]
boxers, briefs	seluar dalam lelaki	[sɛluar dalam lɛlaki]
panties	seluar dalam perempuan	[sɛluar dalam pɛrɛmpuan]
undershirt (A-shirt)	singlet	[siŋlet]
socks	sok	[so]

nightdress	baju tidur	[badʒu tidur]
bra	kutang	[kutaŋ]
knee highs (knee-high socks)	stoking sampai lutut	[stokiŋ sampaj lutut]
pantyhose	sarung kaki	[saruŋ kaki]
stockings (thigh highs)	stoking	[stokiŋ]
bathing suit	pakaian renang	[pakajan rɛnaŋ]

35. Headwear

hat	topi	[topi]
fedora	topi bulat	[topi bulat]
baseball cap	topi besbol	[topi besbol]
flatcap	kep	[kep]

beret	beret	[beret]
hood	hud	[hud]
panama hat	topi panama	[topi panamə]
knit cap (knitted hat)	topi kait	[topi kait]

| headscarf | tudung | [tuduŋ] |
| women's hat | topi perempuan | [topi pɛrɛmpuan] |

hard hat	topi besi	[topi bɛsi]
garrison cap	topi lipat	[topi lipat]
helmet	helmet	[helmet]

| derby | topi bulat | [topi bulat] |
| top hat | topi pesulap | [topi pɛsulap] |

36. Footwear

footwear	kasut	[kasut]
shoes (men's shoes)	but	[but]
shoes (women's shoes)	kasut wanita	[kasut vanitə]

| boots (e.g., cowboy ~) | kasut lars | [kasut lars] |
| slippers | selipar | [slipar] |

tennis shoes (e.g., Nike ~)	kasut tenis	[kasut tenis]
sneakers	kasut kets	[kasut kets]
(e.g., Converse ~)		
sandals	sandal	[sandal]

cobbler (shoe repairer)	tukang kasut	[tukaŋ kasut]
heel	tumit	[tumit]
pair (of shoes)	sepasang	[sɛpasaŋ]

| shoestring | tali kasut | [tali kasut] |
| to lace (vt) | mengikat tali | [meŋikat tali] |

| shoehorn | sudu kasut | [sudu kasut] |
| shoe polish | belaking | [bɛlakiŋ] |

37. Personal accessories

gloves	sarung tangan	[saruŋ taŋan]
mittens	miten	[mitɛn]
scarf (muffler)	selendang	[sɛlendaŋ]

glasses (eyeglasses)	kaca mata	[katʃa matə]
frame (eyeglass ~)	bingkai, rim	[biŋkaj], [rim]
umbrella	payung	[pajuŋ]
walking stick	tongkat	[toŋkat]

| hairbrush | berus rambut | [brus rambut] |
| fan | kipas | [kipas] |

| tie (necktie) | tai | [taj] |
| bow tie | tali leher kupu-kupu | [tali leher kupu kupu] |

| suspenders | tali bawat | [tali bavat] |
| handkerchief | sapu tangan | [sapu taŋan] |

| comb | sikat | [sikat] |
| barrette | cucuk rambut | [tʃutʃuk rambut] |

| hairpin | pin rambut | [pin rambut] |
| buckle | gancu | [gantʃu] |

| belt | ikat pinggang | [ikat piŋgaŋ] |
| shoulder strap | tali beg | [tali beg] |

bag (handbag)	beg	[beg]
purse	beg tangan	[beg taŋan]
backpack	beg galas	[beg galas]

38. Clothing. Miscellaneous

fashion	fesyen	[feʃɛn]
in vogue (adj)	berfesyen	[bɛrfeʃɛn]
fashion designer	pereka fesyen	[pɛreka feʃɛn]

collar	kerah	[krah]
pocket	saku	[saku]
pocket (as adj)	saku	[saku]
sleeve	lengan	[lɛŋan]
hanging loop	gelung sangkut	[gɛluŋ saŋkut]
fly (on trousers)	golbi	[golbi]

zipper (fastener)	zip	[zip]
fastener	kancing	[kantʃiŋ]
button	butang	[butaŋ]
buttonhole	lubang butang	[lubaŋ butaŋ]
to come off (ab. button)	terlepas	[tɛrlɛpas]

to sew (vi, vt)	menjahit	[mɛndʒahit]
to embroider (vi, vt)	menyulam	[mɛnjulam]
embroidery	sulaman	[sulaman]
sewing needle	jarum	[dʒarum]
thread	benang	[bɛnaŋ]
seam	jahitan	[dʒahitan]

to get dirty (vi)	menjadi kotor	[mɛndʒadi kotor]
stain (mark, spot)	tompok	[tompo]
to crease, crumple (vi)	renyuk	[rɛnju]
to tear, to rip (vt)	merobek	[mɛrobe]
clothes moth	gegat	[gɛgat]

39. Personal care. Cosmetics

toothpaste	ubat gigi	[ubat gigi]
toothbrush	berus gigi	[bɛrus gigi]
to brush one's teeth	memberus gigi	[mɛmbɛrus gigi]

razor	pisau cukur	[pisau tʃukur]
shaving cream	krim cukur	[krim tʃukur]
to shave (vi)	bercukur	[bɛrtʃukur]

| soap | sabun | [sabun] |
| shampoo | syampu | [ʃampu] |

scissors	gunting	[guntiŋ]
nail file	kikir kuku	[kikir kuku]
nail clippers	pemotong kuku	[pɛmotoŋ kuku]
tweezers	penyepit kecil	[pɛnjepit kɛtʃil]

cosmetics	**alat solek**	[alat sole]
face mask	**masker**	[maskɛr]
manicure	**manicure**	[mɛnikjur]
to have a manicure	**melakukan perawatan kuku tangan**	[mɛlakukan pɛravatan kuku taŋan]
pedicure	**pedicure**	[pɛdikjur]
make-up bag	**beg mekap**	[beg mekap]
face powder	**bedak**	[bɛda]
powder compact	**kotak bedak**	[kotak bɛda]
blusher	**pemerah pipi**	[pɛmerah pipi]
perfume (bottled)	**minyak wangi**	[minjak vaŋi]
toilet water (lotion)	**air wangi**	[air vaŋi]
lotion	**losen**	[losen]
cologne	**air kolong**	[air koloŋ]
eyeshadow	**pembayang mata**	[pɛmbajaŋ matə]
eyeliner	**pensel kening**	[pensel kɛniŋ]
mascara	**maskara**	[maskarə]
lipstick	**gincu bibir**	[gintʃu bibir]
nail polish, enamel	**pengilat kuku**	[peɲilat kuku]
hair spray	**penyembur rambut**	[pɛnjembur rambut]
deodorant	**deodoran**	[deodoran]
cream	**krim**	[krim]
face cream	**krim muka**	[krim mukə]
hand cream	**krim tangan**	[krim taŋan]
anti-wrinkle cream	**krim antikerut**	[krim antikɛrut]
day cream	**krim siang**	[krim siaŋ]
night cream	**krim malam**	[krim malam]
day (as adj)	**siang**	[siaŋ]
night (as adj)	**malam**	[malam]
tampon	**tampon**	[tampon]
toilet paper (toilet roll)	**kertas tandas**	[kɛrtas tandas]
hair dryer	**pengering rambut**	[peŋeriŋ rambut]

40. Watches. Clocks

watch (wristwatch)	**jam tangan**	[dʒam taŋan]
dial	**permukaan jam**	[permukaan dʒam]
hand (of clock, watch)	**jarum**	[dʒarum]
metal watch band	**gelang jam tangan**	[gɛlaŋ dʒam taŋan]
watch strap	**tali jam**	[tali dʒam]
battery	**bateri**	[batɛri]
to be dead (battery)	**luput**	[luput]
to change a battery	**menukar bateri**	[menukar batɛri]

to run fast	**kecepatan**	[kɛtʃɛpatan]
to run slow	**ketinggalan**	[kɛtiŋgalan]
wall clock	**jam dinding**	[dʒam dindiŋ]
hourglass	**jam pasir**	[dʒam pasir]
sundial	**jam matahari**	[dʒam matahari]
alarm clock	**jam loceng**	[dʒam lotʃeŋ]
watchmaker	**tukang jam**	[tukaŋ dʒam]
to repair (vt)	**membaiki**	[mɛmbaiki]

EVERYDAY EXPERIENCE

T&P Books Publishing

41. Money

money	**wang**	[vaŋ]
currency exchange	**pertukaran**	[pɛrtukaran]
exchange rate	**kadar pertukaran**	[kadar pɛrtukaran]
ATM	**ATM**	[ɛj ti ɛm]
coin	**syiling**	[ʃiliŋ]
dollar	**dolar**	[dolar]
euro	**euro**	[euro]
lira	**lire Itali**	[lirɛ itali]
Deutschmark	**Deutsche Mark**	[dojʧe mar]
franc	**franc**	[fraŋk]
pound sterling	**paun**	[paun]
yen	**yen**	[jen]
debt	**hutang**	[hutaŋ]
debtor	**si berhutang**	[si bɛrhutaŋ]
to lend (money)	**meminjamkan**	[mɛmindʒamkan]
to borrow (vi, vt)	**meminjam**	[mɛmindʒam]
bank	**bank**	[baŋ]
account	**akaun**	[akaun]
to deposit (vt)	**memasukkan**	[mɛmasukkan]
to deposit into the account	**memasukkan ke dalam akaun**	[mɛmasukkan ke dalam akaun]
to withdraw (vt)	**mengeluarkan wang**	[mɛŋɛluarkan vaŋ]
credit card	**kad kredit**	[kad kredit]
cash	**wang tunai**	[vaŋ tunaj]
check	**cek**	[ʧe]
to write a check	**menulis cek**	[mɛnulis ʧe]
checkbook	**buku cek**	[buku ʧe]
wallet	**beg duit**	[beg duit]
change purse	**dompet**	[dompet]
safe	**peti besi**	[pɛti bɛsi]
heir	**pewaris**	[pɛvaris]
inheritance	**warisan**	[varisan]
fortune (wealth)	**kekayaan**	[kɛkajaan]
lease	**sewa**	[sevə]
rent (money)	**sewa rumah**	[sevə rumah]
to rent (sth from sb)	**menyewa**	[mɛnjevə]

128

price	harga	[hargə]
cost	kos	[kos]
sum	jumlah	[dʒumlah]

to spend (vt)	menghabiskan	[mɛŋɣabiskan]
expenses	belanja	[blandʒə]
to economize (vi, vt)	menjimatkan	[mɛndʒimatkan]
economical	cermat	[tʃɛrmat]

to pay (vi, vt)	membayar	[mɛmbajar]
payment	pembayaran	[pɛmbajaran]
change (give the ~)	sisa wang	[sisa vaŋ]

tax	cukai	[tʃukaj]
fine	denda	[dɛndə]
to fine (vt)	mendenda	[mɛndɛndə]

42. Post. Postal service

post office	pejabat pos	[pɛdʒabat pos]
mail (letters, etc.)	mel	[mel]
mailman	posmen	[posmen]
opening hours	waktu pejabat	[vaktu pɛdʒabat]

letter	surat	[surat]
registered letter	surat berdaftar	[surat bɛrdaftar]
postcard	poskad	[poskad]
telegram	telegram	[telegram]
package (parcel)	kiriman pos	[kiriman pos]
money transfer	kiriman wang	[kiriman vaŋ]

to receive (vt)	menerima	[mɛnɛrimə]
to send (vt)	mengirim	[mɛŋirim]
sending	pengiriman	[pɛŋiriman]

address	alamat	[alamat]
ZIP code	poskod	[poskod]
sender	pengirim	[pɛŋirim]
receiver	penerima	[pɛnɛrimə]

| name (first name) | nama | [namə] |
| surname (last name) | nama keluarga | [nama kɛluargə] |

postage rate	tarif	[tarif]
standard (adj)	biasa, lazim	[biasə], [lazim]
economical (adj)	ekonomik	[ekonomi]

weight	berat	[brat]
to weigh (~ letters)	menimbang	[mɛnimbaŋ]
envelope	sampul surat	[sampul surat]

| postage stamp | setem | [sɛtem] |
| to stamp an envelope | melekatkan setem | [mɛlɛkatkan ɛetem] |

43. Banking

| bank | bank | [baŋ] |
| branch (of bank, etc.) | cawangan | [ʧavaŋan] |

| bank clerk, consultant | perunding | [pɛrundiŋ] |
| manager (director) | pengurus | [pɛŋurus] |

bank account	akaun	[akaun]
account number	nombor akaun	[nombor akaun]
checking account	akaun semasa	[akaun sɛmasə]
savings account	akaun simpanan	[akaun simpanan]

| to open an account | membuka akaun | [mɛmbuka akaun] |
| to close the account | menutup akaun | [mɛnutup akaun] |

| to deposit into the account | memasukkan wang ke dalam akaun | [mɛmasukkan vaŋ kɛ dalam akaun] |
| to withdraw (vt) | mengeluarkan wang | [mɛŋɛluarkan vaŋ] |

| deposit | simpanan wang | [simpanan vaŋ] |
| to make a deposit | memasukkan wang | [mɛmasukkan vaŋ] |

| wire transfer | transfer | [transfer] |
| to wire, to transfer | mengirim duit | [mɛŋirim duit] |

| sum | jumlah | [ʤumlah] |
| How much? | Berapa? | [brapə] |

| signature | tanda tangan | [tanda taŋan] |
| to sign (vt) | menandatangani | [mɛnandataŋani] |

| credit card | kad kredit | [kad kredit] |
| code (PIN code) | kod | [kod] |

| credit card number | nombor kad kredit | [nombor kad kredit] |
| ATM | ATM | [ɛj ti ɛm] |

check	cek	[ʧe]
to write a check	menulis cek	[mɛnulis ʧe]
checkbook	buku cek	[buku ʧe]

loan (bank ~)	pinjaman	[pinʤaman]
to apply for a loan	meminta pinjaman	[mɛminta pinʤaman]
to get a loan	mengambil pinjaman	[mɛŋambil pinʤaman]
to give a loan	memberi pinjaman	[mɛmbri pinʤaman]
guarantee	jaminan	[ʤaminan]

44. Telephone. Phone conversation

telephone	**telefon**	[telefon]
cell phone	**telefon bimbit**	[telefon bimbit]
answering machine	**mesin menjawab panggilan telefon**	[mesin mɛndʒavab paŋgilan telefon]
to call (by phone)	**menelefon**	[mɛnelefon]
phone call	**panggilan telefon**	[paŋgilan telefon]
to dial a number	**mendail nombor**	[mɛndajl nombor]
Hello!	**Helo!**	[helo]
to ask (vt)	**menyoal**	[mɛnjoal]
to answer (vi, vt)	**menjawab**	[mɛndʒavab]
to hear (vt)	**mendengar**	[mɛndɛŋar]
well (adv)	**baik**	[bai]
not well (adv)	**buruk**	[buru]
noises (interference)	**bising**	[bisiŋ]
receiver	**gagang**	[gagaŋ]
to pick up (~ the phone)	**mengankat gagang telefon**	[mɛŋaŋkat gagaŋ telefon]
to hang up (~ the phone)	**meletakkan gagang telefon**	[mɛlɛtakkan gagaŋ telefon]
busy (engaged)	**sibuk**	[sibu]
to ring (ab. phone)	**berdering**	[bɛrdɛriŋ]
telephone book	**buku panduan telefon**	[buku panduan telefon]
local (adj)	**tempatan**	[tɛmpatan]
local call	**panggilan tempatan**	[paŋgilan tɛmpatan]
long distance (~ call)	**antarabandar**	[antarabandar]
long-distance call	**panggilan antarabandar**	[paŋgilan antarabandar]
international (adj)	**antarabangsa**	[antarabaŋsə]
international call	**panggilan antarabangsa**	[paŋgilan antarabaŋsə]

45. Cell phone

cell phone	**telefon bimbit**	[telefon bimbit]
display	**peranti paparan**	[pɛranti paparan]
button	**tombol**	[tombol]
SIM card	**Kad SIM**	[kad sim]
battery	**bateri**	[batɛri]
to be dead (battery)	**nyahcas**	[njahtʃas]
charger	**pengecas**	[pɛŋɛtʃas]
menu	**menu**	[menu]
settings	**setting**	[setiŋ]

| tune (melody) | melodi nada dering | [melodi nada dɛriŋ] |
| to select (vt) | memilih | [mɛmilih] |

calculator	mesin hitung	[mesin hituŋ]
voice mail	mesin menjawab panggilan telefon	[mesin mɛndʒavab paŋgilan telefon]
alarm clock	jam loceng	[dʒam lotʃeŋ]
contacts	buku panduan telefon	[buku panduan telefon]

| SMS (text message) | SMS, khidmat pesanan ringkas | [ɛs ɛm ɛs], [hidmat pɛsanan riŋkas] |
| subscriber | pelanggan | [pɛlaŋgan] |

46. Stationery

| ballpoint pen | pena mata bulat | [pɛna mata bulat] |
| fountain pen | pena tinta | [pɛna tintə] |

pencil	pensel	[pensel]
highlighter	pen penyerlah	[pen pɛnjerlah]
felt-tip pen	marker	[marker]

| notepad | buku catatan | [buku tʃatatan] |
| agenda (diary) | buku harian | [buku harian] |

ruler	kayu pembaris	[kaju pɛmbaris]
calculator	mesin hitung	[mesin hituŋ]
eraser	getah pemadam	[gɛtah pɛmadam]
thumbtack	paku tekan	[paku tɛkan]
paper clip	klip kertas	[klip kɛrtas]

glue	perekat	[pɛrɛkat]
stapler	pengokot	[pɛŋokot]
hole punch	penebuk	[pɛnɛbu]
pencil sharpener	pengasah pensel	[pɛŋasah pensel]

47. Foreign languages

language	bahasa	[bahasə]
foreign (adj)	asing	[asiŋ]
foreign language	bahasa asing	[bahasa asiŋ]
to study (vt)	mempelajari	[mɛmpɛladʒari]
to learn (language, etc.)	belajar	[bɛladʒar]

to read (vi, vt)	membaca	[mɛmbatʃə]
to speak (vi, vt)	bercakap	[bɛrtʃakap]
to understand (vt)	memahami	[mɛmahami]
to write (vt)	menulis	[mɛnulis]

fast (adv)	**fasih**	[fasih]
slowly (adv)	**perlahan-lahan**	[pɛrlahan lahan]
fluently (adv)	**fasih**	[fasih]
rules	**peraturan**	[pɛraturan]
grammar	**nahu**	[nahu]
vocabulary	**kosa kata**	[kosa katə]
phonetics	**fonetik**	[foneti]
textbook	**buku teks**	[buku teks]
dictionary	**kamus**	[kamus]
teach-yourself book	**buku teks pembelajaran kendiri**	[buku teks pɛmbɛladʒaran kɛndiri]
phrasebook	**buku ungkapan**	[buku uŋkapan]
cassette, tape	**kaset**	[kaset]
videotape	**kaset video**	[kaset video]
CD, compact disc	**cakera padat**	[tʃakra padat]
DVD	**cakera DVD**	[tʃakra dividi]
alphabet	**abjad**	[abdʒad]
to spell (vt)	**mengeja**	[mɛŋedʒə]
pronunciation	**sebutan**	[sɛbutan]
accent	**aksen**	[aksen]
with an accent	**dengan pelat**	[dɛŋan pelat]
without an accent	**tanpa pelat**	[tanpa pelat]
word	**perkataan**	[pɛrkataan]
meaning	**erti**	[ɛrti]
course (e.g., a French ~)	**kursus**	[kursus]
to sign up	**berdaftar**	[bɛrdaftar]
teacher	**pensyarah**	[pɛnɕarah]
translation (process)	**penterjemahan**	[pɛntɛrdʒemahan]
translation (text, etc.)	**terjemahan**	[tɛrdʒemahan]
translator	**penterjemah**	[pɛntɛrdʒemah]
interpreter	**penterjemah**	[pɛntɛrdʒemah]
polyglot	**penutur pelbagai bahasa**	[pɛnutur pɛlbagaj bahasə]
memory	**ingatan**	[iŋatan]

MEALS. RESTAURANT

T&P Books Publishing

48. Table setting

spoon	sudu	[sudu]
knife	pisau	[pisau]
fork	garpu	[garpu]

cup (e.g., coffee ~)	cawan	[ʧavan]
plate (dinner ~)	pinggan	[piŋgan]
saucer	alas cawan	[alas ʧavan]
napkin (on table)	napkin	[napkin]
toothpick	cungkil gigi	[ʧuŋkil gigi]

49. Restaurant

restaurant	restoran	[restoran]
coffee house	kedai kopi	[kɛdaj kopi]
pub, bar	bar	[bar]
tearoom	ruang teh	[ruaŋ te]

waiter	pelayan	[pɛlajan]
waitress	pelayan perempuan	[pɛlajan pɛrɛmpuan]
bartender	pelayan bar	[pɛlajan bar]
menu	menu	[menu]
wine list	kad wain	[kad vajn]
to book a table	menempah meja	[mɛnɛmpah medʒə]
course, dish	masakan	[masakan]
to order (meal)	menempah	[mɛnɛmpah]
to make an order	menempah	[mɛnɛmpah]

aperitif	aperitif	[aperitif]
appetizer	pembuka selera	[pɛmbuka sɛlerə]
dessert	pencuci mulut	[pɛnʧuʧi mulut]

check	bil	[bil]
to pay the check	membayar bil	[mɛmbajar bil]
to give change	memberi wang baki	[mɛmbri vaŋ baki]
tip	tip	[tip]

50. Meals

food	makanan	[makanan]
to eat (vi, vt)	makan	[makan]

breakfast	makan pagi	[makan pagi]
to have breakfast	makan pagi	[makan pagi]
lunch	makan tengah hari	[makan tɛŋah hari]
to have lunch	makan tengah hari	[makan tɛŋah hari]
dinner	makan malam	[makan malam]
to have dinner	makan malam	[makan malam]

| appetite | selera | [sɛlerə] |
| Enjoy your meal! | Selamat jamu selera! | [sɛlamat dʒamu sɛlerə] |

to open (~ a bottle)	membuka	[mɛmbukə]
to spill (liquid)	menumpahkan	[mɛnumpahkan]
to spill out (vi)	tertumpah	[tɛrtumpah]

to boil (vi)	mendidih	[mɛndidih]
to boil (vt)	mendidihkan	[mɛndidihkan]
boiled (~ water)	masak	[masa]
to chill, cool down (vt)	menyejukkan	[mɛnjedʒukkan]
to chill (vi)	menjadi sejuk	[mɛndʒadi sɛdʒu]

| taste, flavor | rasa | [rasə] |
| aftertaste | rasa kesan | [rasa kɛsan] |

to slim down (lose weight)	berdiet	[berdiet]
diet	diet	[diet]
vitamin	vitamin	[vitamin]
calorie	kalori	[kalori]
vegetarian (n)	vegetarian	[vegetarian]
vegetarian (adj)	vegetarian	[vegetarian]

fats (nutrient)	lemak	[lɛma]
proteins	protein	[protein]
carbohydrates	karbohidrat	[karbohidrat]

slice (of lemon, ham)	irisan	[irisan]
piece (of cake, pie)	potongan	[potoŋan]
crumb	remah	[remah]
(of bread, cake, etc.)		

51. Cooked dishes

course, dish	hidangan	[hidaŋan]
cuisine	masakan	[masakan]
recipe	resipi	[rɛsipi]
portion	hidangan	[hidaŋan]

salad	salad	[salad]
soup	sup	[sup]
clear soup (broth)	sup kosong	[sup kosoŋ]
sandwich (bread)	sandwic	[sandvitʃ]

fried eggs	telur mata kerbau	[tɛlur mata kerbau]
hamburger (beefburger)	hamburger	[hamburger]
beefsteak	stik	[sti]

side dish	garnish	[garniʃ]
spaghetti	spaghetti	[spaɣeti]
mashed potatoes	kentang lecek	[kɛntaŋ letʃe]
pizza	piza	[pizə]
porridge (oatmeal, etc.)	bubur	[bubur]
omelet	telur dadar	[tɛlur dadar]

boiled (e.g., ~ beef)	rebus	[rɛbus]
smoked (adj)	salai	[salaj]
fried (adj)	goreng	[goreŋ]
dried (adj)	dikeringkan	[dikɛriŋkan]
frozen (adj)	sejuk beku	[sɛdʒuk bɛku]
pickled (adj)	dijeruk	[didʒɛru]

sweet (sugary)	manis	[manis]
salty (adj)	masin	[masin]
cold (adj)	sejuk	[sɛdʒu]
hot (adj)	panas	[panas]
bitter (adj)	pahit	[pahit]
tasty (adj)	sedap	[sɛdap]

to cook in boiling water	merebus	[mɛrɛbus]
to cook (dinner)	memasak	[mɛmasa]
to fry (vt)	menggoreng	[mɛŋgoreŋ]
to heat up (food)	memanaskan	[mɛmanaskan]

to salt (vt)	membubuh garam	[mɛmbubuh garam]
to pepper (vt)	membubuh lada	[mɛmbubuh ladə]
to grate (vt)	memarut	[mɛmarut]
peel (n)	kulit	[kulit]
to peel (vt)	mengupas	[mɛŋupas]

52. Food

meat	daging	[dagiŋ]
chicken	ayam	[ajam]
Rock Cornish hen (poussin)	anak ayam	[anak ajam]
duck	itik	[iti]
goose	angsa	[aŋsə]
game	burung buruan	[buruŋ buruan]
turkey	ayam belanda	[ajam blandə]

pork	daging babi	[dagiŋ babi]
veal	daging anak lembu	[dagiŋ anak lembu]
lamb	daging bebiri	[dagiŋ bɛbiri]

| beef | daging lembu | [daɡiŋ lɛmbu] |
| rabbit | arnab | [arnab] |

sausage (bologna, etc.)	sosej worst	[sosedʒ vorst]
vienna sausage (frankfurter)	sosej	[sosedʒ]
bacon	dendeng babi	[deŋdeŋ babi]
ham	ham	[ham]
gammon	gamon	[gamon]

pâté	pate	[patɛ]
liver	hati	[hati]
hamburger (ground beef)	bahan kisar	[bahan kisar]
tongue	lidah	[lidah]

egg	telur	[tɛlur]
eggs	telur-telur	[tɛlur tɛlur]
egg white	putih telur	[putih tɛlur]
egg yolk	kuning telur	[kuniŋ tɛlur]

fish	ikan	[ikan]
seafood	makanan laut	[makanan laut]
crustaceans	krustasia	[krustasiə]
caviar	caviar	[kaviar]

crab	ketam	[kɛtam]
shrimp	udang	[udaŋ]
oyster	tiram	[tiram]
spiny lobster	udang krai	[udaŋ kraj]
octopus	sotong	[sotoŋ]
squid	cumi-cumi	[tʃumi tʃumi]

sturgeon	ikan sturgeon	[ikan sturgeon]
salmon	salmon	[salmon]
halibut	ikan halibut	[ikan halibut]

cod	ikan kod	[ikan kod]
mackerel	ikan tenggiri	[ikan tɛngiri]
tuna	tuna	[tunə]
eel	ikan keli	[ikan kli]

trout	ikan trout	[ikan trout]
sardine	sadin	[sadin]
pike	ikan paik	[ikan paj]
herring	ikan hering	[ikan hɛriŋ]

bread	roti	[roti]
cheese	keju	[kɛdʒu]
sugar	gula	[gulə]
salt	garam	[garam]
rice	beras, nasi	[bras], [nasi]
pasta (macaroni)	pasta	[pastə]

noodles	mie	[mi]
butter	mentega	[mɛntegə]
vegetable oil	minyak sayur	[minjak sajur]
sunflower oil	minyak bunga matahari	[minjak buŋa matahari]
margarine	marjerin	[mardʒɛrin]

| olives | buah zaitun | [buah zajtun] |
| olive oil | minyak zaitun | [minjak zaɪtun] |

milk	susu	[susu]
condensed milk	susu pekat	[susu pɛkat]
yogurt	yogurt	[jogurt]
sour cream	krim asam	[krim asam]
cream (of milk)	krim	[krim]

| mayonnaise | mayonis | [majonis] |
| buttercream | krim | [krim] |

groats (barley ~, etc.)	bijirin berkupas	[bidʒirin bɛrkupas]
flour	tepung	[tɛpuŋ]
canned food	makanan dalam tin	[makanan dalam tin]

cornflakes	emping jagung	[ɛmpiŋ dʒaguŋ]
honey	madu	[madu]
jam	jem	[dʒɛm]
chewing gum	gula-gula getah	[gula gula gɛtah]

53. Drinks

water	air	[air]
drinking water	air minum	[air minum]
mineral water	air galian	[air galian]

still (adj)	tanpa gas	[tanpa gas]
carbonated (adj)	bergas	[bɛrgas]
sparkling (adj)	bergas	[bɛrgas]
ice	ais	[ajs]
with ice	dengan ais	[dɛŋan ajs]

non-alcoholic (adj)	tanpa alkohol	[tanpa alkohol]
soft drink	minuman ringan	[minuman riŋan]
refreshing drink	minuman segar	[minuman sɛgar]
lemonade	limonad	[limonad]

liquors	arak	[ara]
wine	wain	[vajn]
white wine	wain putih	[vajn putih]
red wine	wain merah	[vajn merah]
liqueur	likur	[likur]
champagne	champagne	[ʃampejn]

vermouth	vermouth	[vermut]
whiskey	wiski	[viski]
vodka	vodka	[vodkə]
gin	gin	[dʒin]
cognac	cognac	[konjak]
rum	rum	[ram]

coffee	kopi	[kopi]
black coffee	kopi O	[kopi o]
coffee with milk	kopi susu	[kopi susu]
cappuccino	cappuccino	[kaputʃino]
instant coffee	kopi segera	[kopi sɛgɛrə]

milk	susu	[susu]
cocktail	koktel	[koktel]
milkshake	susu kocak	[susu kotʃa]

juice	jus	[dʒus]
tomato juice	jus tomato	[dʒus tomato]
orange juice	jus jeruk manis	[dʒus dʒɛruk manis]
freshly squeezed juice	jus segar	[dʒus sɛgar]

beer	bir	[bir]
light beer	bir putih	[bir putih]
dark beer	bir hitam	[bir hitam]

tea	teh	[te]
black tea	teh hitam	[te hitam]
green tea	teh hijau	[te hidʒau]

54. Vegetables

| vegetables | sayuran | [sajuran] |
| greens | ulam-ulaman | [ulam ulaman] |

tomato	tomato	[tomato]
cucumber	timun	[timun]
carrot	lobak merah	[lobak merah]
potato	kentang	[kɛntaŋ]
onion	bawang	[bavaŋ]
garlic	bawang putih	[bavaŋ putih]

cabbage	kubis	[kubis]
cauliflower	bunga kubis	[buŋa kubis]
Brussels sprouts	kubis Brussels	[kubis brasels]
broccoli	broccoli	[brokoli]

beet	rut bit	[rut bit]
eggplant	terung	[tɛruŋ]
zucchini	labu kuning	[labu kuniŋ]

| pumpkin | labu | [labu] |
| turnip | turnip | [turnip] |

parsley	parsli	[parsli]
dill	jintan hitam	[dʒintan hitam]
lettuce	pokok salad	[pokok salad]
celery	saderi	[sadɛri]
asparagus	asparagus	[asparagus]
spinach	bayam	[bajam]

pea	kacang sepat	[katʃaŋ sɛpat]
beans	kacang	[katʃaŋ]
corn (maize)	jagung	[dʒaguŋ]
kidney bean	kacang buncis	[katʃaŋ buntʃis]

bell pepper	lada	[ladə]
radish	lobak	[loba]
artichoke	articok	[artitʃo]

55. Fruits. Nuts

fruit	buah	[buah]
apple	epal	[epal]
pear	buah pear	[buah pear]
lemon	lemon	[lemon]
orange	jeruk manis	[dʒeruk manis]
strawberry (garden ~)	strawberi	[stroberi]

mandarin	limau mandarin	[limau mandarin]
plum	plum	[plam]
peach	pic	[pitʃ]
apricot	aprikot	[aprikot]
raspberry	raspberi	[rasberi]
pineapple	nanas	[nanas]

banana	pisang	[pisaŋ]
watermelon	tembikai	[tembikaj]
grape	anggur	[aŋgur]
sour cherry	buah ceri	[buah tʃeri]
sweet cherry	ceri manis	[tʃeri manis]
melon	tembikai susu	[tembikaj susu]

grapefruit	limau gedang	[limau gɛdaŋ]
avocado	avokado	[avokado]
papaya	betik	[bɛti]
mango	mempelam	[mɛmpɛlam]
pomegranate	buah delima	[buah dɛlimə]

| redcurrant | buah kismis merah | [buah kismis merah] |
| blackcurrant | buah kismis hitam | [buah kismis hitam] |

gooseberry	buah gusberi	[buah gusberi]
bilberry	buah bilberi	[buah bilberi]
blackberry	beri hitam	[beri hitam]

raisin	kismis	[kismis]
fig	buah tin	[buah tin]
date	buah kurma	[buah kurmə]

peanut	kacang tanah	[katʃaŋ tanah]
almond	badam	[badam]
walnut	walnut	[volnat]
hazelnut	kacang hazel	[katʃaŋ hazel]
coconut	buah kelapa	[buah klapə]
pistachios	pistasio	[pistasio]

56. Bread. Candy

bakers' confectionery (pastry)	kuih-muih	[kuih muih]
bread	roti	[roti]
cookies	biskit	[biskit]

chocolate (n)	coklat	[tʃoklat]
chocolate (as adj)	coklat	[tʃoklat]
candy (wrapped)	gula-gula	[gula gulə]
cake (e.g., cupcake)	kuih	[kuih]
cake (e.g., birthday ~)	kek	[ke]

| pie (e.g., apple ~) | pai | [paj] |
| filling (for cake, pie) | inti | [inti] |

jam (whole fruit jam)	jem buah-buahan utuh	[dʒem buah buahan utuh]
marmalade	marmalad	[marmalad]
wafers	wafer	[vafɛr]
ice-cream	ais krim	[ajs krim]
pudding	puding	[pudiŋ]

57. Spices

salt	garam	[garam]
salty (adj)	masin	[masin]
to salt (vt)	membubuh garam	[mɛmbubuh garam]

black pepper	lada hitam	[lada hitam]
red pepper (milled ~)	lada merah	[lada merah]
mustard	sawi	[savi]
horseradish	remunggai	[rɛmuŋgaj]
condiment	perasa	[pɛrasə]

spice	rempah-rempah	[rempah rempah]
sauce	saus	[saus]
vinegar	cuka	[ʧukə]

anise	lawang	[lavaŋ]
basil	kemangi	[kɛmaɲi]
cloves	cengkeh	[ʧeŋkeh]
ginger	halia	[haliə]
coriander	ketumbar	[kɛtumbar]
cinnamon	kayu manis	[kaju manis]

sesame	bijan	[biʤan]
bay leaf	daun bay	[daun bej]
paprika	paprik	[papri]
caraway	jintan putih	[ʤintan putih]
saffron	safron	[safron]

PERSONAL INFORMATION. FAMILY

T&P Books Publishing

58. Personal information. Forms

name (first name)	**nama**	[namə]
surname (last name)	**nama keluarga**	[nama kɛluargə]
date of birth	**tarikh lahir**	[tarih lahir]
place of birth	**tempat lahir**	[tɛmpat lahir]
nationality	**bangsa**	[baŋsə]
place of residence	**tempat kediaman**	[tɛmpat kediaman]
country	**negara**	[nɛgarə]
profession (occupation)	**profesion**	[profesion]
gender, sex	**jenis kelamin**	[dʒɛnis kɛlamin]
height	**tinggi badan**	[tiŋgi badan]
weight	**berat**	[brat]

59. Family members. Relatives

mother	**ibu**	[ibu]
father	**bapa**	[bapə]
son	**anak lelaki**	[anak lɛlaki]
daughter	**anak perempuan**	[anak pɛrɛmpuan]
younger daughter	**anak perempuan bungsu**	[anak pɛrɛmpuan buŋsu]
younger son	**anak lelali bungsu**	[anak lɛlali buŋsu]
eldest daughter	**anak perempuan sulung**	[anak pɛrɛmpuan suluŋ]
eldest son	**anak lelaki sulung**	[anak lɛlaki suluŋ]
brother	**saudara**	[saudarə]
elder brother	**abang**	[abaŋ]
younger brother	**adik lelaki**	[adik lɛlaki]
sister	**saudara perempuan**	[saudara pɛrɛmpuan]
elder sister	**kakak perempuan**	[kakak pɛrɛmpuan]
younger sister	**adik perempuan**	[adik pɛrɛmpuan]
cousin (masc.)	**sepupu lelaki**	[sɛpupu lɛlaki]
cousin (fem.)	**sepupu perempuan**	[sɛpupu pɛrɛmpuan]
mom, mommy	**ibu**	[ibu]
dad, daddy	**bapa**	[bapə]
parents	**ibu bapa**	[ibu bapə]
child	**anak**	[ana]
children	**anak-anak**	[anak ana]
grandmother	**nenek**	[nene]
grandfather	**datuk**	[datu]

grandson	cucu lelaki	[ʧuʧu lɛlaki]
granddaughter	cucu perempuan	[ʧuʧu pɛrɛmpuan]
grandchildren	cucu-cicit	[ʧuʧu ʧiʧit]

uncle	pak cik	[pak ʧi]
aunt	mak cik	[mak ʧi]
nephew	anak saudara lelaki	[anak saudara lɛlaki]
niece	anak saudara perempuan	[anak saudara pɛrɛmpuan]

mother-in-law (wife's mother)	ibu mertua	[ibu mɛrtuə]
father-in-law (husband's father)	bapa mertua	[bapa mɛrtuə]
son-in-law (daughter's husband)	menantu lelaki	[mɛnantu lɛlaki]
stepmother	ibu tiri	[ibu tiri]
stepfather	bapa tiri	[bapa tiri]
infant	bayi	[baji]
baby (infant)	bayi	[baji]
little boy, kid	budak kecil	[budak kɛʧil]

wife	isteri	[istri]
husband	suami	[suami]
spouse (husband)	suami	[suami]
spouse (wife)	isteri	[istri]

married (masc.)	berkahwin, beristeri	[bɛrkahvin], [bɛristri]
married (fem.)	berkahwin, bersuami	[bɛrkahvin], [bɛrsuami]
single (unmarried)	bujang	[budʒaŋ]
bachelor	bujang	[budʒaŋ]
divorced (masc.)	bercerai	[bɛrʧɛraj]
widow	balu	[balu]
widower	duda	[dudə]

relative	saudara	[saudarə]
close relative	keluarga dekat	[kɛluarga dɛkat]
distant relative	saudara jauh	[saudara dʒauh]
relatives	keluarga	[kɛluargə]

orphan (boy or girl)	piatu	[piatu]
guardian (of a minor)	wali	[vali]
to adopt (a boy)	mengangkat anak lelaki	[mɛŋaŋkat anak lɛlaki]
to adopt (a girl)	mengangkat anak perempuan	[mɛŋaŋkat anak pɛrɛmpuan]

60. Friends. Coworkers

| friend (masc.) | sahabat | [sahabat] |
| friend (fem.) | teman wanita | [tɛman vanitə] |

| friendship | persahabatan | [pɛrsahabatan] |
| to be friends | bersahabat | [bɛrsahabat] |

buddy (masc.)	teman	[tɛman]
buddy (fem.)	teman wanita	[tɛman vanitə]
partner	rakan	[rakan]

chief (boss)	bos	[bos]
superior (n)	kepala	[kɛpalə]
owner, proprietor	pemilik	[pɛmili]
subordinate (n)	orang bawahan	[oraŋ bavahan]
colleague	rakan	[rakan]

acquaintance (person)	kenalan	[kɛnalan]
fellow traveler	rakan seperjalanan	[rakan sɛpɛrdʒalanan]
classmate	teman sedarjah	[tɛman sɛdardʒah]

neighbor (masc.)	jiran lelaki	[dʒiran lɛlaki]
neighbor (fem.)	jiran perempuan	[dʒiran pɛrɛmpuan]
neighbors	jiran	[dʒiran]

HUMAN BODY. MEDICINE

T&P Books Publishing

61. Head

head	**kepala**	[kɛpalə]
face	**muka**	[mukə]
nose	**hidung**	[hiduŋ]
mouth	**mulut**	[mulut]
eye	**mata**	[matə]
eyes	**mata**	[matə]
pupil	**anak mata**	[anak matə]
eyebrow	**kening**	[kɛniŋ]
eyelash	**bulu mata**	[bulu matə]
eyelid	**kekopak mata**	[kɛkopak matə]
tongue	**lidah**	[lidah]
tooth	**gigi**	[gigi]
lips	**bibir**	[bibir]
cheekbones	**tulang pipi**	[tulaŋ pipi]
gum	**gusi**	[gusi]
palate	**lelangit**	[lɛlaŋit]
nostrils	**lubang hidung**	[lubaŋ hiduŋ]
chin	**dagu**	[dagu]
jaw	**rahang**	[rahaŋ]
cheek	**pipi**	[pipi]
forehead	**dahi**	[dahi]
temple	**pelipis**	[pɛlipis]
ear	**telinga**	[tɛliŋə]
back of the head	**tengkuk**	[tɛŋku]
neck	**leher**	[leher]
throat	**kerongkong**	[kɛroŋkoŋ]
hair	**rambut**	[rambut]
hairstyle	**potongan rambut**	[potoŋan rambut]
haircut	**potongan rambut**	[potoŋan rambut]
wig	**rambut palsu, wig**	[rambut palsu], [vig]
mustache	**misai**	[misaj]
beard	**janggut**	[dʒaŋgut]
to have (a beard, etc.)	**memelihara**	[mɛmɛliharə]
braid	**tocang**	[totʃaŋ]
sideburns	**jambang**	[dʒambaŋ]
red-haired (adj)	**berambut merah perang**	[bɛrambut mɛrah peraŋ]
gray (hair)	**beruban**	[bɛruban]

bald (adj)	botak	[bota]
bald patch	botak	[bota]
ponytail	ikat ekor kuda	[ikat ekor kudə]
bangs	jambul	[dʒambul]

62. Human body

hand	tangan	[taŋan]
arm	lengan	[lɛŋan]
finger	jari	[dʒari]
toe	jari	[dʒari]
thumb	ibu jari	[ibu dʒari]
little finger	jari kelengkeng	[dʒari kɛleŋkŋ]
nail	kuku	[kuku]
fist	penumbuk	[pɛnumbu]
palm	telapak	[tɛlapa]
wrist	pergelangan	[pɛrgɛlaŋan]
forearm	lengan bawah	[lɛŋan bavah]
elbow	siku	[siku]
shoulder	bahu	[bahu]
leg	kaki	[kaki]
foot	telapak kaki	[telapak kaki]
knee	lutut	[lutut]
calf (part of leg)	betis	[bɛtis]
hip	paha	[pahə]
heel	tumit	[tumit]
body	badan	[badan]
stomach	perut	[prut]
chest	dada	[dadə]
breast	tetek	[tete]
flank	rusuk	[rusu]
back	belakang	[blakaŋ]
lower back	pinggul	[piŋgul]
waist	pinggang	[piŋgaŋ]
navel (belly button)	pusat	[pusat]
buttocks	punggung	[puŋguŋ]
bottom	punggung	[puŋguŋ]
beauty mark	tahi lalat manis	[tahi lalat manis]
birthmark (café au lait spot)	tanda kelahiran	[tanda kɛlahiran]
tattoo	tatu	[tatu]
scar	bekas luka	[bɛkas lukə]

63. Diseases

sickness	penyakit	[pɛnjakit]
to be sick	sakit	[sakit]
health	kesihatan	[kɛsihatan]

runny nose (coryza)	hidung berair	[hiduŋ bɛrair]
tonsillitis	radang tenggorok	[radaŋ tɛŋgoro]
cold (illness)	selesema	[sɛlsɛmə]
to catch a cold	demam selesema	[dɛmam sɛlsɛmə]

bronchitis	bronkitis	[broŋkitis]
pneumonia	radang paru-paru	[radaŋ paru paru]
flu, influenza	selesema	[sɛlsɛmə]

nearsighted (adj)	rabun jauh	[rabun dʒauh]
farsighted (adj)	rabun dekat	[rabun dɛkat]
strabismus (crossed eyes)	mata juling	[mata dʒuliŋ]
cross-eyed (adj)	bermata juling	[bɛrmata dʒuliŋ]
cataract	katarak	[katara]
glaucoma	glaukoma	[glaukomə]

stroke	angin amhar	[aŋin amhar]
heart attack	serangan jantung	[sɛraŋan dʒantuŋ]
myocardial infarction	serangan jantung	[sɛraŋan dʒantuŋ]
paralysis	lumpuh	[lumpuh]
to paralyze (vt)	melumpuhkan	[mɛlumpuhkan]

allergy	alahan	[alahan]
asthma	penyakit lelah	[pɛnjakit lɛlah]
diabetes	diabetes	[diabetes]

| toothache | sakit gigi | [sakit gigi] |
| caries | karies | [karis] |

diarrhea	cirit-birit	[tʃirit birit]
constipation	sembelit	[sɛmbɛlit]
stomach upset	sakit perut	[sakit prut]
food poisoning	keracunan	[kɛratʃunan]
to get food poisoning	keracunan	[kɛratʃunan]

arthritis	artritis	[artritis]
rickets	penyakit riket	[pɛnjakit riket]
rheumatism	reumatisme	[reumatismɛ]
atherosclerosis	aterosklerosis	[aterosklerosis]

gastritis	gastritis	[gastritis]
appendicitis	apendisitis	[apendisitis]
cholecystitis	radang pundi hempedu	[radaŋ pundi hɛmpɛdu]
ulcer	ulser	[ulser]
measles	campak	[tʃampa]

rubella (German measles)	**penyakit campak Jerman**	[pɛnjakit tʃampak dʒerman]
jaundice	**sakit kuning**	[sakit kuniŋ]
hepatitis	**hepatitis**	[hepatitis]
schizophrenia	**skizofrenia**	[skizofreniə]
rabies (hydrophobia)	**penyakit anjing gila**	[pɛnjakit andʒiŋ gilə]
neurosis	**neurosis**	[neurosis]
concussion	**gegaran otak**	[gɛgaran ota]
cancer	**barah, kanser**	[barah], [kansɛr]
sclerosis	**sklerosis**	[sklerosis]
multiple sclerosis	**sklerosis berbilang**	[sklerosis bɛrbilaŋ]
alcoholism	**alkoholisme**	[alkoholismɛ]
alcoholic (n)	**kaki arak**	[kaki ara]
syphilis	**sifilis**	[sifilis]
AIDS	**AIDS**	[ejds]
tumor	**tumor**	[tumor]
malignant (adj)	**ganas**	[ganas]
benign (adj)	**bukan barah**	[bukan barah]
fever	**demam**	[dɛmam]
malaria	**malaria**	[malariə]
gangrene	**kelemayuh**	[kɛlɛmajuh]
seasickness	**mabuk laut**	[mabuk laut]
epilepsy	**epilepsi**	[epilepsi]
epidemic	**wabak**	[vaba]
typhus	**tifus**	[tifus]
tuberculosis	**tuberkulosis**	[tubɛrkulosis]
cholera	**penyakit taun**	[pɛnjakit taun]
plague (bubonic ~)	**sampar**	[sampar]

64. Symptoms. Treatments. Part 1

symptom	**tanda**	[tandə]
temperature	**suhu**	[suhu]
high temperature (fever)	**suhu tinggi**	[suhu tiŋgi]
pulse (heartbeat)	**nadi**	[nadi]
dizziness (vertigo)	**rasa pening**	[rasa pɛniŋ]
hot (adj)	**panas**	[panas]
shivering	**gigil**	[gigil]
pale (e.g., ~ face)	**pucat**	[putʃat]
cough	**batuk**	[batu]
to cough (vi)	**batuk**	[batu]
to sneeze (vi)	**bersin**	[bɛrsin]
faint	**pengsan**	[peŋsan]

to faint (vi)	**jatuh pengsan**	[dʒatuh peŋsan]
bruise (hématome)	**luka lebam**	[luka lɛbam]
bump (lump)	**bengkak**	[bɛŋka]
to bang (bump)	**melanggar**	[mɛlaŋgar]
contusion (bruise)	**luka memar**	[luka mɛmar]
to get a bruise	**kena luka memar**	[kɛna luka mɛmar]
to limp (vi)	**berjalan pincang**	[bɛrdʒalan pintʃaŋ]
dislocation	**seliuh**	[sɛliuh]
to dislocate (vt)	**terseliuh**	[tɛrsɛliuh]
fracture	**patah**	[patah]
to have a fracture	**patah**	[patah]
cut (e.g., paper ~)	**hirisan**	[hirisan]
to cut oneself	**terhiris**	[tɛrhiris]
bleeding	**pendarahan**	[pɛndarahan]
burn (injury)	**luka bakar**	[luka bakar]
to get burned	**terkena luka bakar**	[tɛrkɛna luka bakar]
to prick (vt)	**mencucuk**	[mɛntʃutʃu]
to prick oneself	**tercucuk**	[tɛrtʃutʃu]
to injure (vt)	**mencedera**	[mntʃɛdɛrə]
injury	**cedera**	[tʃɛdɛrə]
wound	**cedera**	[tʃɛdɛrə]
trauma	**trauma**	[traumə]
to be delirious	**meracau**	[mɛratʃau]
to stutter (vi)	**gagap**	[gagap]
sunstroke	**strok matahari**	[strok matahari]

65. Symptoms. Treatments. Part 2

pain, ache	**sakit**	[sakit]
splinter (in foot, etc.)	**selumbar**	[sɛlumbar]
sweat (perspiration)	**peluh**	[pɛluh]
to sweat (perspire)	**berpeluh**	[bɛrpɛluh]
vomiting	**muntah**	[muntah]
convulsions	**kekejangan**	[kɛkɛdʒaŋan]
pregnant (adj)	**hamil**	[hamil]
to be born	**dilahirkan**	[dilahirkan]
delivery, labor	**kelahiran**	[kɛlahiran]
to deliver (~ a baby)	**melahirkan**	[mɛlahirkan]
abortion	**pengguguran anak**	[pɛŋguguran ana]
breathing, respiration	**pernafasan**	[pɛrnafasan]
in-breath (inhalation)	**tarikan nafas**	[tarikan nafas]
out-breath (exhalation)	**penghembusan nafas**	[pɛŋɣɛmbusan nafas]

| to exhale (breathe out) | menghembuskan nafas | [mɛɲɛmbuskan nafas] |
| to inhale (vi) | menarik nafas | [mɛnarik nafas] |

disabled person	orang kurang upaya	[oraŋ kuraŋ upajə]
cripple	orang kurang upaya	[oraŋ kuraŋ upajə]
drug addict	penagih dadah	[pɛnagih dadah]

deaf (adj)	tuli	[tuli]
mute (adj)	bisu	[bisu]
deaf mute (adj)	bisu tuli	[bisu tuli]

mad, insane (adj)	gila	[gilə]
madman (demented person)	lelaki gila	[lɛlaki gilə]
madwoman	perempuan gila	[pɛrɛmpuan gilə]
to go insane	menjadi gila	[mɛndʒadi gilə]

gene	gen	[gen]
immunity	kekebalan	[kɛkɛbalan]
hereditary (adj)	pusaka, warisan	[pusakə], [varisan]
congenital (adj)	bawaan	[bavaan]

virus	virus	[virus]
microbe	kuman	[kuman]
bacterium	kuman	[kuman]
infection	jangkitan	[dʒaŋkitan]

66. Symptoms. Treatments. Part 3

| hospital | hospital | [hospital] |
| patient | pesakit | [pɛsakit] |

diagnosis	diagnosis	[diagnosis]
cure	rawatan	[ravatan]
medical treatment	rawatan	[ravatan]
to get treatment	berubat	[bɛrubat]
to treat (~ a patient)	merawat	[mɛravat]
to nurse (look after)	merawat	[mɛravat]
care (nursing ~)	jagaan	[dʒagaan]

operation, surgery	pembedahan, surgeri	[pɛmbɛdahan], ['sødʒeri]
to bandage (head, limb)	membalut	[membalut]
bandaging	pembalutan	[pɛmbalutan]

vaccination	suntikan	[suntikan]
to vaccinate (vt)	menanam cacar	[mɛnanam tʃatʃar]
injection, shot	cucukan, injeksi	[tʃutʃukan], [indʒeksi]
to give an injection	membuat suntikan	[mɛmbuat suntikan]
attack	serangan	[sɛraŋan]
amputation	pemotongan	[pɛmotoŋan]

to amputate (vt)	memotong	[mɛmotoŋ]
coma	keadaan koma	[kɛadaan komə]
to be in a coma	dalam keadaan koma	[dalam kɛadaan komə]
intensive care	rawatan rapi	[ravatan rapi]

to recover (~ from flu)	sembuh	[sɛmbuh]
condition (patient's ~)	keadaan	[kɛadaan]
consciousness	kesedaran	[kɛsedaran]
memory (faculty)	ingatan	[iŋatan]

to pull out (tooth)	mencabut	[mɛntʃabut]
filling	tampal gigi	[tampal gigi]
to fill (a tooth)	menampal	[mɛnampal]

| hypnosis | hipnosis | [hipnosis] |
| to hypnotize (vt) | menghipnosis | [mɛŋɣipnosis] |

67. Medicine. Drugs. Accessories

medicine, drug	ubat	[ubat]
remedy	ubat	[ubat]
to prescribe (vt)	mempreskripsikan	[mɛmpreskripsikan]
prescription	preskripsi	[preskripsi]

tablet, pill	pil	[pil]
ointment	ubat sapu	[ubat sapu]
ampule	ampul	[ampul]
mixture, solution	ubat cair	[ubat tʃair]
syrup	sirup	[sirup]
capsule	pil	[pil]
powder	serbuk	[sɛrbu]

gauze bandage	kain pembalut	[kain pɛmbalut]
cotton wool	kapas	[kapas]
iodine	iodin	[iodin]

| Band-Aid | plaster | [plastɛr] |
| eyedropper | pipet | [pipet] |

| thermometer | meter suhu | [metɛr suhu] |
| syringe | picagari | [pitʃagari] |

| wheelchair | kerusi roda | [krusi rodə] |
| crutches | tongkat ketiak | [toŋkat kɛtia] |

painkiller	ubat penahan sakit	[ubat pɛnahan sakit]
laxative	julap	[dʒulap]
spirits (ethanol)	alkohol	[alkohol]
medicinal herbs	herba perubatan	[hɛrba pɛrubatan]
herbal (~ tea)	herba	[hɛrbə]

APARTMENT

T&P Books Publishing

68. Apartment

apartment	**pangsapuri**	[paŋsapuri]
room	**bilik**	[bili]
bedroom	**bilik tidur**	[bilik tidur]
dining room	**bilik makan**	[bilik makan]
living room	**ruang tamu**	[ruaŋ tamu]
study (home office)	**bilik bacaan**	[bilik batʃaan]
entry room	**ruang depan**	[ruaŋ dɛpan]
bathroom (room with a bath or shower)	**bilik mandi**	[bilik mandi]
half bath	**tandas**	[tandas]
ceiling	**siling**	[siliŋ]
floor	**lantai**	[lantaj]
corner	**sudut**	[sudut]

69. Furniture. Interior

furniture	**perabot**	[pɛrabot]
table	**meja**	[medʒə]
chair	**kerusi**	[krusi]
bed	**katil**	[katil]
couch, sofa	**sofa**	[sofə]
armchair	**kerusi tangan**	[krusi taŋan]
bookcase	**almari buku**	[almari buku]
shelf	**rak**	[ra]
wardrobe	**almari**	[almari]
coat rack (wall-mounted ~)	**tempat sangkut baju**	[tɛmpat saŋkut badʒu]
coat stand	**penyangkut kot**	[pɛnjaŋkut kot]
bureau, dresser	**almari laci**	[almari latʃi]
coffee table	**meja tamu**	[medʒa tamu]
mirror	**cermin**	[tʃɛrmin]
carpet	**permaidani**	[pɛrmajdani]
rug, small carpet	**ambal**	[ambal]
fireplace	**perapian**	[pɛrapian]
candle	**linlin**	[linlin]
candlestick	**kaki dian**	[kaki dian]

drapes	langsir	[laŋsir]
wallpaper	kertas dinding	[kɛrtas dindiŋ]
blinds (jalousie)	kerai	[kraj]

table lamp	lampu meja	[lampu medʒə]
wall lamp (sconce)	lampu dinding	[lampu dindiŋ]
floor lamp	lampu lantai	[lampu lantaj]
chandelier	candelier	[tʃandelir]

leg (of chair, table)	kaki	[kaki]
armrest	lengan	[lɛŋan]
back (backrest)	sandaran	[sandaran]
drawer	laci	[latʃi]

70. Bedding

bedclothes	linen	[linen]
pillow	bantal	[bantal]
pillowcase	sarung bantal	[saruŋ bantal]
duvet, comforter	selimut	[sɛlimut]
sheet	kain cadar	[kain tʃadar]
bedspread	tutup tilam bantal	[tutup tilam bantal]

71. Kitchen

kitchen	dapur	[dapur]
gas	gas	[gas]
gas stove (range)	dapur gas	[dapur gas]
electric stove	dapur elektrik	[dapur elektri]
oven	oven	[oven]
microwave oven	dapur gelombang mikro	[dapur gɛlombaŋ mikro]

refrigerator	peti sejuk	[pɛti sɛdʒu]
freezer	petak sejuk beku	[petak sɛdʒuk bɛku]
dishwasher	mesin basuh pinggan mangkuk	[mesin basuh piŋgan maŋku]

meat grinder	pengisar daging	[pɛŋisar dagiŋ]
juicer	pemerah jus	[pɛmɛrah dʒus]
toaster	pembakar roti	[pɛmbakar roti]
mixer	pengadun	[pɛŋadun]

coffee machine	pembuat kopi	[pɛmbuat kopi]
coffee pot	kole kopi	[kole kopi]
coffee grinder	pengisar kopi	[pɛŋisar kopi]

| kettle | cerek | [tʃere] |
| teapot | poci | [potʃi] |

| lid | **tutup** | [tutup] |
| tea strainer | **penapis the** | [pɛnapis teh] |

spoon	**sudu**	[sudu]
teaspoon	**sudu teh**	[sudu teh]
soup spoon	**sudu makan**	[sudu makan]
fork	**garpu**	[garpu]
knife	**pisau**	[pisau]

tableware (dishes)	**pinggan mangkuk**	[piŋgan maŋku]
plate (dinner ~)	**pinggan**	[piŋgan]
saucer	**alas cawan**	[alas tʃavan]

shot glass	**gelas wain kecil**	[glas vajn ketʃil]
glass (tumbler)	**gelas**	[glas]
cup	**cawan**	[tʃavan]

sugar bowl	**tempat gula**	[tɛmpat gulə]
salt shaker	**tempat garam**	[tɛmpat garam]
pepper shaker	**tempat lada**	[tɛmpat ladə]
butter dish	**tempat mentega**	[tɛmpat mɛntegə]

stock pot (soup pot)	**periuk**	[priu]
frying pan (skillet)	**kuali**	[kuali]
ladle	**sendok**	[sendo]
colander	**alat peniris**	[alat pɛniris]
tray (serving ~)	**dulang**	[dulaŋ]

bottle	**botol**	[botol]
jar (glass)	**balang**	[balaŋ]
can	**tin**	[tin]

bottle opener	**pembuka botol**	[pɛmbuka botol]
can opener	**pembuka tin**	[pɛmbuka tin]
corkscrew	**skru gabus**	[skru gabus]
filter	**penapis**	[pɛnapis]
to filter (vt)	**menapis**	[mɛnapis]

| trash, garbage (food waste, etc.) | **sampah** | [sampah] |
| trash can (kitchen ~) | **baldi sampah** | [baldi sampah] |

72. Bathroom

bathroom	**bilik mandi**	[bilik mandi]
water	**air**	[air]
faucet	**pili**	[pili]
hot water	**air panas**	[air panas]
cold water	**air sejuk**	[air sɛdʒu]
toothpaste	**ubat gigi**	[ubat gigi]

to brush one's teeth	memberus gigi	[mɛmbɛrus gigi]
toothbrush	berus gigi	[bɛrus gigi]
to shave (vi)	bercukur	[bɛrtʃukur]
shaving foam	buih cukur	[buih tʃukur]
razor	pisau cukur	[pisau tʃukur]
to wash (one's hands, etc.)	mencuci	[mɛntʃutʃi]
to take a bath	mandi	[mandi]
shower	pancuran mandi	[pantʃuran mandi]
to take a shower	mandi di bawah pancuran air	[mandi di bavah pantʃuran air]
bathtub	tab mandi	[tab mandi]
toilet (toilet bowl)	mangkuk tandas	[maŋkuk tandas]
sink (washbasin)	sink cuci tangan	[siŋk tʃutʃi taŋan]
soap	sabun	[sabun]
soap dish	tempat sabun	[tɛmpat sabun]
sponge	span	[span]
shampoo	syampu	[ʃampu]
towel	tuala	[tualə]
bathrobe	jubah mandi	[dʒubah mandi]
laundry (laundering)	pembasuhan	[pɛmbasuhan]
washing machine	mesin pembasuh	[mesin pɛmbasuh]
to do the laundry	membasuh	[mɛmbasuh]
laundry detergent	serbuk pencuci	[serbuk pɛntʃutʃi]

73. Household appliances

TV set	peti televisyen	[pɛti televiʃɛn]
tape recorder	perakam	[pɛrakam]
VCR (video recorder)	perakam video	[pɛrakam video]
radio	pesawat radio	[pɛsavat radio]
player (CD, MP3, etc.)	pemain	[pɛmajn]
video projector	penayang video	[pɛnajaŋ video]
home movie theater	pawagam rumah	[pavagam rumah]
DVD player	pemain DVD	[pɛmajn di vi di]
amplifier	penguat	[pɛŋwat]
video game console	konsol permainan video	[konsol pɛrmajnan video]
video camera	kamera video	[kamera video]
camera (photo)	kamera foto	[kamera foto]
digital camera	kamera digital	[kamera digital]
vacuum cleaner	pembersih vakum	[pɛmbɛrsih vakum]
iron (e.g., steam ~)	seterika	[sɛtɛrikə]

ironing board	**papan seterika**	[papan sɛtɛrikə]
telephone	**telefon**	[telefon]
cell phone	**telefon bimbit**	[telefon bimbit]
typewriter	**mesin taip**	[mesin tajp]
sewing machine	**mesin jahit**	[mesin dʒahit]
microphone	**mikrofon**	[mikrofon]
headphones	**pendengar telinga**	[pɛndɛŋar tɛliŋə]
remote control (TV)	**alat kawalan jauh**	[alat kavalan dʒauh]
CD, compact disc	**cakera padat**	[tʃakra padat]
cassette, tape	**kaset**	[kaset]
vinyl record	**piring hitam**	[piriŋ hitam]

THE EARTH. WEATHER

T&P Books Publishing

space	angkasa lepas	[aŋkasa lɛpas]
space (as adj)	angkasa lepas	[aŋkasa lɛpas]
outer space	ruang angkasa lepas	[ruaŋ aŋkasa lɛpas]
world	dunia	[duniə]
universe	alam semesta	[alam sɛmɛstə]
galaxy	Bimasakti	[bimasakti]
star	bintang	[bintaŋ]
constellation	gugusan bintang	[gugusan bintaŋ]
planet	planet	[planet]
satellite	satelit	[satɛlit]
meteorite	meteorit	[meteorit]
comet	komet	[komet]
asteroid	asteroid	[asteroid]
orbit	edaran, orbit	[edaran], [orbit]
to revolve	berputar	[bɛrputar]
(~ around the Earth)		
atmosphere	udara	[udarə]
the Sun	Matahari	[matahari]
solar system	tata surya	[tata surjə]
solar eclipse	gerhana matahari	[gɛrhana matahari]
the Earth	Bumi	[bumi]
the Moon	Bulan	[bulan]
Mars	Marikh	[mariχ]
Venus	Zuhrah	[zuhrah]
Jupiter	Musytari	[muʃtari]
Saturn	Zuhal	[zuhal]
Mercury	Utarid	[utarid]
Uranus	Uranus	[uranus]
Neptune	Waruna	[varunə]
Pluto	Pluto	[pluto]
Milky Way	Bima Sakti	[bima sakti]
Great Bear (Ursa Major)	Bintang Biduk	[bintaŋ bidu]
North Star	Bintang Utara	[bintaŋ utarə]
Martian	makhluk dari Marikh	[mahluk dari marih]
extraterrestrial (n)	makhluk ruang angkasa	[maχluk ruaŋ aŋkasə]

alien	**makhluk asing**	[mahluk asiŋ]
flying saucer	**piring terbang**	[piriŋ tɛrbaŋ]
spaceship	**kapal angkasa lepas**	[kapal aŋkasa lɛpas]
space station	**stesen orbit angkasa**	[stesen orbit aŋkasə]
blast-off	**pelancaran**	[pɛlantʃaran]
engine	**enjin**	[endʒin]
nozzle	**muncung**	[muntʃuŋ]
fuel	**bahan bakar**	[bahan bakar]
cockpit, flight deck	**kokpit**	[kokpit]
antenna	**aerial**	[aerial]
porthole	**tingkap kapal**	[tiŋkap kapal]
solar panel	**sel surya**	[sel surjə]
spacesuit	**pakaian angkasawan**	[pakajan aŋkasavan]
weightlessness	**keadaan graviti sifar**	[kɛadaan graviti sifar]
oxygen	**oksigen**	[oksigɛn]
docking (in space)	**percantuman**	[pɛrtʃantuman]
to dock (vi, vt)	**melakukan cantuman**	[mɛlakukan tʃantuman]
observatory	**balai cerap**	[balaj tʃɛrap]
telescope	**teleskop**	[teleskop]
to observe (vt)	**menyaksikan**	[mɛnjaksikan]
to explore (vt)	**menjelajahi**	[mɛndʒɛladʒahi]

75. The Earth

the Earth	**Bumi**	[bumi]
the globe (the Earth)	**bola Bumi**	[bola bumi]
planet	**planet**	[planet]
atmosphere	**udara**	[udarə]
geography	**geografi**	[geografi]
nature	**alam**	[alam]
globe (table ~)	**glob**	[glob]
map	**peta**	[pɛtə]
atlas	**atlas**	[atlas]
Europe	**Eropah**	[eropə]
Asia	**Asia**	[asiə]
Africa	**Afrika**	[afrikə]
Australia	**Australia**	[australiə]
America	**Amerika**	[amerikə]
North America	**Amerika Utara**	[amerika utarə]
South America	**Amerika Selatan**	[amerika sɛlatan]

| Antarctica | **Antartika** | [antartikə] |
| the Arctic | **Artik** | [arti] |

76. Cardinal directions

north	**utara**	[utarə]
to the north	**ke utara**	[kɛ utarə]
in the north	**di utara**	[di utarə]
northern (adj)	**utara**	[utarə]

south	**selatan**	[sɛlatan]
to the south	**ke selatan**	[kɛ sɛlatan]
in the south	**di selatan**	[di sɛlatan]
southern (adj)	**selatan**	[sɛlatan]

west	**barat**	[barat]
to the west	**ke barat**	[kɛ barat]
in the west	**di barat**	[di barat]
western (adj)	**barat**	[barat]

east	**timur**	[timur]
to the east	**ke timur**	[kɛ timur]
in the east	**di timur**	[di timur]
eastern (adj)	**timur**	[timur]

77. Sea. Ocean

sea	**laut**	[laut]
ocean	**lautan**	[lautan]
gulf (bay)	**teluk**	[tɛlu]
straits	**selat**	[sɛlat]

| land (solid ground) | **daratan** | [daratan] |
| continent (mainland) | **benua** | [bɛnuə] |

island	**pulau**	[pulau]
peninsula	**semenanjung**	[sɛmɛnandʒuŋ]
archipelago	**kepulauan**	[kɛpulawan]

bay, cove	**teluk**	[tɛlu]
harbor	**pelabuhan**	[pɛlabuhan]
lagoon	**lagun**	[lagun]
cape	**tanjung**	[tandʒuŋ]

atoll	**pulau cincin**	[pulau tʃintʃin]
reef	**terumbu**	[tɛrumbu]
coral	**karang**	[karaŋ]
coral reef	**terumbu karang**	[tɛrumbu karaŋ]

deep (adj)	dalam	[dalam]
depth (deep water)	kedalaman	[kɛdalaman]
abyss	jurang	[dʒuraŋ]
trench (e.g., Mariana ~)	jurang	[dʒuraŋ]

| current (Ocean ~) | arus | [arus] |
| to surround (bathe) | bersempadan | [bɛrsɛmpadan] |

| shore | pantai | [pantaj] |
| coast | pantai | [pantaj] |

flow (flood tide)	air pasang	[air pasaŋ]
ebb (ebb tide)	air surut	[air surut]
shoal	beting	[bɛtiŋ]
bottom (~ of the sea)	dasar	[dasar]

wave	gelombang	[gɛlombaŋ]
crest (~ of a wave)	puncak gelombang	[puntʃak gɛlombaŋ]
spume (sea foam)	buih	[buih]

storm (sea storm)	badai	[badaj]
hurricane	badai, taufan	[badaj], [taufan]
tsunami	tsunami	[tsunami]
calm (dead ~)	angin mati	[aŋin mati]
quiet, calm (adj)	tenang	[tɛnaŋ]

| pole | khutub | [χutub] |
| polar (adj) | polar | [polar] |

latitude	garisan lintang	[garisan lintaŋ]
longitude	garisan bujur	[garisan budʒur]
parallel	garisan latitud	[garisan latitud]
equator	khatulistiwa	[χatulistivə]

sky	langit	[laŋit]
horizon	kaki langit	[kaki laŋit]
air	udara	[udarə]

lighthouse	rumah api	[rumah api]
to dive (vi)	menyelam	[mɛnjelam]
to sink (ab. boat)	karam	[karam]
treasures	harta karun	[harta karun]

78. Seas' and Oceans' names

Atlantic Ocean	Lautan Atlantik	[lautan atlanti]
Indian Ocean	Lautan Hindia	[lautan hindiə]
Pacific Ocean	Lautan Teduh	[lautan tɛduh]
Arctic Ocean	Lautan Arktik	[lautan arkti]
Black Sea	Laut Hitam	[laut hitam]

Red Sea	**Laut Merah**	[laut merah]
Yellow Sea	**Laut Kuning**	[laut kuniŋ]
White Sea	**Laut Putih**	[laut putih]

Caspian Sea	**Laut Caspian**	[laut kaspian]
Dead Sea	**Laut Mati**	[laut mati]
Mediterranean Sea	**Laut Tengah**	[laut tɛŋah]

| Aegean Sea | **Laut Aegean** | [laut idʒian] |
| Adriatic Sea | **Laut Adriatik** | [laut adriati] |

Arabian Sea	**Laut Arab**	[laut arab]
Sea of Japan	**Laut Jepun**	[laut dʒepun]
Bering Sea	**Laut Bering**	[laut beriŋ]
South China Sea	**Laut Cina Selatan**	[laut tʃina sɛlatan]

Coral Sea	**Laut Coral**	[laut koral]
Tasman Sea	**Laut Tasmania**	[laut tasmaniə]
Caribbean Sea	**Laut Caribbean**	[laut karibean]

| Barents Sea | **Laut Barents** | [laut barenʦ] |
| Kara Sea | **Laut Kara** | [laut karə] |

North Sea	**Laut Utara**	[laut utarə]
Baltic Sea	**Laut Baltik**	[laut balti]
Norwegian Sea	**Laut Norway**	[laut norvej]

79. Mountains

mountain	**gunung**	[gunuŋ]
mountain range	**banjaran gunung**	[bandʒaran gunuŋ]
mountain ridge	**rabung gunung**	[rabuŋ gunuŋ]

summit, top	**puncak**	[puntʃa]
peak	**puncak**	[puntʃa]
foot (~ of the mountain)	**kaki**	[kaki]
slope (mountainside)	**cerun**	[tʃerun]

volcano	**gunung berapi**	[gunuŋ bɛrapi]
active volcano	**gunung berapi hidup**	[gunuŋ bɛrapi hidup]
dormant volcano	**gunung api yang tidak aktif**	[gunuŋ api jaŋ tidak aktif]

eruption	**letusan**	[lɛtusan]
crater	**kawah**	[kavah]
magma	**magma**	[magmə]
lava	**lahar**	[lahar]
molten (~ lava)	**pijar**	[pidʒar]
canyon	**kanyon**	[kanjon]
gorge	**jurang**	[dʒuraŋ]

crevice	krevis	[krevis]
abyss (chasm)	jurang	[dʒuraŋ]
pass, col	genting	[gɛntiŋ]
plateau	penara	[pɛnarə]
cliff	cenuram	[ʧɛnuram]
hill	bukit	[bukit]
glacier	glasier	[glasier]
waterfall	air terjun	[air tɛrdʒun]
geyser	pancutan air panas	[panʧutan air panas]
lake	tasik	[tasi]
plain	dataran	[dataran]
landscape	pemandangan	[pɛmandaŋan]
echo	kumandang	[kumandaŋ]
alpinist	pendaki gunung	[pɛndaki gunuŋ]
rock climber	pendaki batu	[pɛndaki batu]
to conquer (in climbing)	menaklukkan	[mɛnaklukkan]
climb (an easy ~)	pendakian	[pɛndakian]

80. Mountains names

The Alps	Alps	[alps]
Mont Blanc	Mont Blanc	[mont blaŋk]
The Pyrenees	Pyrenees	[pirinis]
The Carpathians	Pegunungan Carpathia	[pɛgunuŋan karpatiə]
The Ural Mountains	Pegunungan Ural	[pɛgunuŋan ural]
The Caucasus Mountains	Kaukasia	[kaukasiə]
Mount Elbrus	Elbrus	[elbrus]
The Altai Mountains	Altai	[altaj]
The Tian Shan	Tien Shan	[tien ʃan]
The Pamir Mountains	Pamir	[pamir]
The Himalayas	Himalaya	[himalajə]
Mount Everest	Everest	[everest]
The Andes	Andes	[andes]
Mount Kilimanjaro	Kilimanjaro	[kilimandʒaro]

81. Rivers

river	sungai	[suŋaj]
spring (natural source)	mata air	[mata air]
riverbed (river channel)	dasar sungai	[dasar suŋaj]
basin (river valley)	lembah sungai	[lɛmbah suŋaj]

to flow into …	**bermuara**	[bɛrmuarə]
tributary	**anak sungai**	[anak suŋaj]
bank (of river)	**tepi**	[tepi]

current (stream)	**arus**	[arus]
downstream (adv)	**ke hilir**	[kɛ hilir]
upstream (adv)	**ke hulu**	[kɛ hulu]

inundation	**banjir**	[bandʒir]
flooding	**air bah**	[air bah]
to overflow (vi)	**meluap**	[mɛluap]
to flood (vt)	**menggenangi**	[mɛŋgɛnaŋi]

| shallow (shoal) | **beting** | [bɛtiŋ] |
| rapids | **jeram** | [dʒɛram] |

dam	**empangan**	[ɛmpaŋan]
canal	**terusan**	[tɛrusan]
reservoir (artificial lake)	**takungan**	[takuŋan]
sluice, lock	**pintu air**	[pintu air]

water body (pond, etc.)	**kolam**	[kolam]
swamp (marshland)	**bencah**	[bɛntʃah]
bog, marsh	**paya**	[pajə]
whirlpool	**pusaran air**	[pusaran air]

stream (brook)	**anak sungai**	[anak suŋaj]
drinking (ab. water)	**minum**	[minum]
fresh (~ water)	**tawar**	[tavar]

ice	**ais**	[ajs]
to freeze over	**membeku**	[mɛmbɛku]
(ab. river, etc.)		

82. Rivers' names

| Seine | **Seine** | [sɛn] |
| Loire | **Loire** | [luar] |

Thames	**Thames**	[tɛms]
Rhine	**Rhine**	[rajn]
Danube	**Danube**	[danub]

Volga	**Volga**	[volgə]
Don	**Don**	[don]
Lena	**Lena**	[lenə]

Yellow River	**Hwang Ho**	[hvaŋ ho]
Yangtze	**Yangtze**	[jaŋtze]
Mekong	**Mekong**	[mekoŋ]

Ganges	**Ganges**	[gandʒis]
Nile River	**sungai Nil**	[suŋaj nil]
Congo River	**Congo**	[koŋo]
Okavango River	**Okavango**	[okavaŋo]
Zambezi River	**Zambezi**	[zambezi]
Limpopo River	**Limpopo**	[limpopo]
Mississippi River	**Mississippi**	[misisipi]

83. Forest

forest, wood	**hutan**	[hutan]
forest (as adj)	**hutan**	[hutan]
thick forest	**hutan lebat**	[hutan lɛbat]
grove	**hutan kecil**	[hutan kɛtʃil]
forest clearing	**cerang**	[tʃɛraŋ]
thicket	**belukar**	[bɛlukar]
scrubland	**pokok renek**	[pokok rene]
footpath (troddenpath)	**jalan setapak**	[dʒalan sɛtapa]
gully	**gaung**	[gauŋ]
tree	**pokok**	[poko]
leaf	**daun**	[daun]
leaves (foliage)	**daun-daunan**	[daun daunan]
fall of leaves	**daun luruh**	[daun luruh]
to fall (ab. leaves)	**gugur**	[gugur]
top (of the tree)	**puncak**	[puntʃa]
branch	**cabang**	[tʃabaŋ]
bough	**dahan**	[dahan]
bud (on shrub, tree)	**mata tunas**	[mata tunas]
needle (of pine tree)	**jejarum**	[dʒɛdʒarum]
pine cone	**buah konifer**	[buah konifer]
tree hollow	**lubang**	[lubaŋ]
nest	**sarang**	[saraŋ]
burrow (animal hole)	**lubang**	[lubaŋ]
trunk	**batang**	[bataŋ]
root	**akar**	[akar]
bark	**kulit**	[kulit]
moss	**lumut**	[lumut]
to uproot (remove trees or tree stumps)	**mencabut**	[mɛntʃabut]
to chop down	**menebang**	[mɛnɛbaŋ]
to deforest (vt)	**membasmi hutan**	[mɛmbasmi hutan]

tree stump	tunggul	[tuŋgul]
campfire	unggun api	[uŋgun api]
forest fire	kebakaran	[kɛbakaran]
to extinguish (vt)	memadamkan	[mɛmadamkan]

forest ranger	renjer hutan	[rendʒɛr hutan]
protection	perlindungan	[pɛrlinduŋan]
to protect (~ nature)	melindungi	[mɛlinduŋi]
poacher	penebang haram	[pɛnɛbaŋ haram]
steel trap	perangkap	[praŋkap]

| to gather, to pick (vt) | memetik | [mɛmɛti] |
| to lose one's way | sesat jalan | [sɛsat dʒalan] |

84. Natural resources

natural resources	kekayaan alam	[kɛkajaan alam]
minerals	galian	[galian]
deposits	mendapan	[mɛndapan]
field (e.g., oilfield)	lapangan	[lapaŋan]

to mine (extract)	melombong	[mɛlombɔŋ]
mining (extraction)	perlombongan	[pɛrlombɔŋan]
ore	bijih	[bidʒih]
mine (e.g., for coal)	lombong	[lombɔŋ]
shaft (mine ~)	lombong	[lombɔŋ]
miner	buruh lombong	[buruh lombɔŋ]

| gas (natural ~) | gas | [gas] |
| gas pipeline | talian paip gas | [talian pajp gas] |

oil (petroleum)	minyak	[minja]
oil pipeline	saluran paip minyak	[saluran paɪp minja]
oil well	telaga minyak	[tɛlaga minja]
derrick (tower)	menara minyak	[mɛnara minja]
tanker	kapal tangki	[kapal taŋki]

sand	pasir	[pasir]
limestone	kapur	[kapur]
gravel	kerikil	[kɛrikil]
peat	gambut	[gambut]
clay	tanah liat	[tanah liat]
coal	arang	[araŋ]

iron (ore)	besi	[bɛsi]
gold	emas	[ɛmas]
silver	perak	[pera]
nickel	nikel	[nikɛl]
copper	tembaga	[tɛmbagə]
zinc	zink	[ziŋ]

manganese	mangan	[maŋan]
mercury	air raksa	[air raksə]
lead	timah hitam	[timah hitam]
mineral	galian	[galian]
crystal	hablur	[hablur]
marble	pualam	[pualam]
uranium	uranium	[uranium]

85. Weather

weather	cuaca	[tʃuatʃə]
weather forecast	ramalan cuaca	[ramalan tʃuatʃə]
temperature	suhu	[suhu]
thermometer	termometer	[tɛrmometɛr]
barometer	barometer	[barometɛr]
humid (adj)	lembap	[lɛmbap]
humidity	kelembapan	[kɛlɛmbapan]
heat (extreme ~)	panas terik	[panas tɛri]
hot (torrid)	panas terik	[panas tɛri]
it's hot	panas	[panas]
it's warm	panas	[panas]
warm (moderately hot)	hangat	[haŋat]
it's cold	cuaca sejuk	[tʃuatʃa sɛdʒu]
cold (adj)	sejuk	[sɛdʒu]
sun	matahari	[matahari]
to shine (vi)	bersinar	[bɛrsinar]
sunny (day)	cerah	[tʃɛrah]
to come up (vi)	terbit	[tɛrbit]
to set (vi)	duduk	[dudu]
cloud	awan	[avan]
cloudy (adj)	berawan	[bɛravan]
rain cloud	awan mendung	[avan mɛnduŋ]
somber (gloomy)	mendung	[mɛnduŋ]
rain	hujan	[hudʒan]
it's raining	hujan turun	[hudʒan turun]
rainy (~ day, weather)	hujan	[hudʒan]
to drizzle (vi)	renyai-renyai	[rɛnjai rɛnjai]
pouring rain	hujan lebat	[hudʒan lɛbat]
downpour	hujan lebat	[hudʒan lɛbat]
heavy (e.g., ~ rain)	lebat	[lɛbat]
puddle	lopak	[lopa]

to get wet (in rain)	**kebasahan**	[kɛbasahan]
fog (mist)	**kabus**	[kabus]
foggy	**berkabus**	[bɛrkabus]
snow	**salji**	[salʤi]
it's snowing	**salji turun**	[salʤi turun]

86. Severe weather. Natural disasters

thunderstorm	**hujan ribut**	[huʤan ribut]
lightning (~ strike)	**kilat**	[kilat]
to flash (vi)	**berkilau**	[bɛrkilau]
thunder	**guruh**	[guruh]
to thunder (vi)	**bergemuruh**	[bɛrgɛmuruh]
it's thundering	**guruh berbunyi**	[guruh bɛrbunji]
hail	**hujan batu**	[huʤan batu]
it's hailing	**hujan batu turun**	[huʤan batu turun]
to flood (vt)	**menggenangi**	[mɛŋgɛnaŋi]
flood, inundation	**banjir**	[banʤir]
earthquake	**gempa bumi**	[gɛmpa bumi]
tremor, shoke	**gegaran**	[gɛgaran]
epicenter	**titik**	[titi]
eruption	**letusan**	[lɛtusan]
lava	**lahar**	[lahar]
twister	**puting beliung**	[putiŋ bɛliuŋ]
tornado	**tornado**	[tornado]
typhoon	**taufan**	[taufan]
hurricane	**badai, taufan**	[badaj], [taufan]
storm	**badai**	[badaj]
tsunami	**tsunami**	[ʦunami]
cyclone	**siklon**	[siklon]
bad weather	**cuaca buruk**	[ʧuaʧa buru]
fire (accident)	**kebakaran**	[kɛbakaran]
disaster	**bencana**	[bɛnʧanə]
meteorite	**meteorit**	[meteorit]
avalanche	**runtuhan**	[runtuhan]
snowslide	**salji runtuh**	[salʤi runtuh]
blizzard	**badai salji**	[badaj salʤi]
snowstorm	**ribut salji**	[ribut salʤi]

FAUNA

T&P Books Publishing

87. Mammals. Predators

predator	**pemangsa**	[pɛmaŋsə]
tiger	**harimau**	[harimau]
lion	**singa**	[siŋə]
wolf	**serigala**	[srigalə]
fox	**rubah**	[rubah]
jaguar	**jaguar**	[dʒaguar]
leopard	**harimau akar**	[harimau akar]
cheetah	**harimau bintang**	[harimau bintaŋ]
black panther	**harimau kumbang**	[harimau kumbaŋ]
puma	**puma**	[pumə]
snow leopard	**harimau bintang salji**	[harimau bintaŋ saldʒi]
lynx	**lynx**	[liŋks]
coyote	**koyote**	[kojot]
jackal	**jakal**	[dʒakal]
hyena	**dubuk**	[dubu]

88. Wild animals

animal	**binatang**	[binataŋ]
beast (animal)	**binatang liar**	[binataŋ liar]
squirrel	**tupai**	[tupaj]
hedgehog	**landak susu**	[landak susu]
hare	**kelinci**	[kɛlintʃi]
rabbit	**arnab**	[arnab]
badger	**telugu**	[tɛlugu]
raccoon	**rakun**	[rakun]
hamster	**hamster**	[hamster]
marmot	**marmot**	[marmot]
mole	**tikus tanah**	[tikus tanah]
mouse	**mencit**	[mɛntʃit]
rat	**tikus mondok**	[tikus mondo]
bat	**kelawar**	[kɛlavar]
ermine	**ermin**	[ermin]
sable	**sable**	[sable]
marten	**marten**	[marten]

| weasel | wesel | [vesel] |
| mink | mink | [miŋ] |

| beaver | beaver | [biver] |
| otter | memerang | [mɛmɛraŋ] |

horse	kuda	[kudə]
moose	rusa elk	[rusa el]
deer	rusa	[rusə]
camel	unta	[untə]

bison	bison	[bison]
wisent	aurochs	[oroks]
buffalo	kerbau	[kɛrbau]

zebra	kuda belang	[kuda bɛlaŋ]
antelope	antelop	[antelop]
roe deer	kijang	[kidʒaŋ]
fallow deer	rusa	[rusə]
chamois	chamois	[ʃɛmvə]
wild boar	babi hutan jantan	[babi hutan dʒantan]

whale	ikan paus	[ikan paus]
seal	anjing laut	[andʒiŋ laut]
walrus	walrus	[valrus]
fur seal	anjing laut berbulu	[andʒiŋ laut bɛrbulu]
dolphin	lumba-lumba	[lumba lumbə]

bear	beruang	[bɛruaŋ]
polar bear	beruang kutub	[bɛruaŋ kutub]
panda	panda	[pandə]

monkey	monyet	[monjet]
chimpanzee	cimpanzi	[tʃimpanzi]
orangutan	orang hutan	[oraŋ hutan]
gorilla	gorila	[gorilə]
macaque	kera	[krə]
gibbon	ungka	[uŋkə]

| elephant | gajah | [gadʒah] |
| rhinoceros | badak | [bada] |

| giraffe | zirafah | [zirafah] |
| hippopotamus | kuda air | [kuda air] |

| kangaroo | kanggaru | [kaŋgaru] |
| koala (bear) | koala | [koalə] |

mongoose	cerpelai	[tʃɛrpelaj]
chinchilla	chinchilla	[tʃintʃillə]
skunk	skunk	[skuŋ]
porcupine	landak	[landa]

89. Domestic animals

cat	kucing betina	[kutʃiŋ bɛtinə]
tomcat	kucing jantan	[kutʃiŋ dʒantan]
dog	anjing	[andʒiŋ]
horse	kuda	[kudə]
stallion (male horse)	kuda jantan	[kuda dʒantan]
mare	kuda betina	[kuda bɛtinə]
cow	lembu	[lɛmbu]
bull	lembu jantan	[lɛmbu dʒantan]
ox	lembu jantan	[lɛmbu dʒantan]
sheep (ewe)	kambing biri-biri	[kambiŋ biri biri]
ram	biri-biri jantan	[biri biri dʒantan]
goat	kambing betina	[kambiŋ bɛtinə]
billy goat, he-goat	kambing jantan	[kambiŋ dʒantan]
donkey	keldai	[kɛldaj]
mule	baghal	[baɣal]
pig, hog	babi	[babi]
piglet	anak babi	[anak babi]
rabbit	arnab	[arnab]
hen (chicken)	ayam	[ajam]
rooster	ayam jantan	[ajam dʒantan]
duck	itik	[iti]
drake	itik jantan	[itik dʒantan]
goose	angsa	[aŋsə]
tom turkey, gobbler	ayam belanda jantan	[ajam blanda dʒantan]
turkey (hen)	ayam belanda betina	[ajam blanda bɛtinə]
domestic animals	binatang ternakan	[binataŋ tɛrnakan]
tame (e.g., ~ hamster)	jinak	[dʒina]
to tame (vt)	menjinak	[mɛndʒina]
to breed (vt)	memelihara	[mɛmɛliharə]
farm	ladang, estet	[ladaŋ], [estet]
poultry	ayam-itik	[ajam iti]
cattle	ternakan	[tɛrnakan]
herd (cattle)	kawanan	[kavanan]
stable	kandang kuda	[kandaŋ kudə]
pigpen	kandang babi	[kandaŋ babi]
cowshed	kandang lembu	[kandaŋ lɛmbu]
rabbit hutch	sangkar arnab	[saŋkar arnab]
hen house	kandang ayam	[kandaŋ ajam]

90. Birds

bird	**burung**	[buruŋ]
pigeon	**burung merpati**	[buruŋ mɛrpati]
sparrow	**burung pipit**	[buruŋ pipit]
tit (great tit)	**burung tit**	[buruŋ tit]
magpie	**murai**	[muraj]
raven	**burung raven**	[buruŋ raven]
crow	**burung gagak**	[buruŋ gaga]
jackdaw	**burung jackdaw**	[buruŋ dʒɛkdo]
rook	**burung rook**	[buruŋ ru]
duck	**itik**	[iti]
goose	**angsa**	[aŋsə]
pheasant	**burung kuang**	[buruŋ kuaŋ]
eagle	**helang**	[hɛlaŋ]
hawk	**burung helang**	[buruŋ hɛlaŋ]
falcon	**burung falcon**	[buruŋ falkon]
vulture	**hering**	[hɛriŋ]
condor (Andean ~)	**kondor**	[kondor]
swan	**swan**	[svon]
crane	**burung jenjang**	[buruŋ dʒɛndʒaŋ]
stork	**burung botak**	[buruŋ bota]
parrot	**burung nuri**	[buruŋ nuri]
hummingbird	**burung madu**	[buruŋ madu]
peacock	**burung merak**	[buruŋ mɛra]
ostrich	**burung unta**	[buruŋ untə]
heron	**burung pucung**	[buruŋ putʃuŋ]
flamingo	**burung flamingo**	[buruŋ flamiŋo]
pelican	**burung undan**	[buruŋ undan]
nightingale	**burung merbah**	[buruŋ mɛrbah]
swallow	**burung layang-layang**	[buruŋ lajaŋ lajaŋ]
thrush	**burung murai**	[buruŋ muraj]
song thrush	**burung song thrush**	[buruŋ soŋ traʃ]
blackbird	**burung hitam**	[buruŋ hitam]
swift	**burung walet**	[buruŋ valet]
lark	**seri ayu**	[sri aju]
quail	**burung puyuh**	[buruŋ pujuh]
woodpecker	**burung belatuk**	[buruŋ bɛlatu]
cuckoo	**sewah padang**	[sɛvah padaŋ]
owl	**burung hantu**	[buruŋ hantu]
eagle owl	**burung jampok**	[buruŋ dʒampo]

wood grouse	wood grouse	[vud graus]
black grouse	grouse hitam	[graus hitam]
partridge	ayam hutan	[ajam hutan]

starling	burung starling	[buruŋ starliŋ]
canary	burung kenari	[buruŋ kɛnari]
hazel grouse	burung hazel grouse	[buruŋ hazel graus]
chaffinch	burung chaffinch	[buruŋ tʃafintʃ]
bullfinch	burung bullfinch	[buruŋ bulfintʃ]

seagull	burung camar	[buruŋ tʃamar]
albatross	albatros	[albatros]
penguin	penguin	[peŋuin]

91. Fish. Marine animals

bream	ikan bream	[ikan brim]
carp	ikan kap	[ikan kap]
perch	ikan puyu	[ikan puju]
catfish	ikan keli	[ikan kli]
pike	ikan paik	[ikan paj]

| salmon | salmon | [salmon] |
| sturgeon | ikan sturgeon | [ikan sturgeon] |

herring	ikan hering	[ikan hɛriŋ]
Atlantic salmon	salmon Atlantik	[salmon atlanti]
mackerel	ikan tenggiri	[ikan tɛŋgiri]
flatfish	ikan sebelah	[ikan sɛblah]

zander, pike perch	ikan zander	[ikan zander]
cod	ikan kod	[ikan kod]
tuna	tuna	[tunə]
trout	ikan trout	[ikan trout]

eel	ikan belut	[ikan bɛlut]
electric ray	ikan pari elektrik	[ikan pari ɛlektri]
moray eel	ikan moray eel	[ikan morej il]
piranha	pirana	[piranə]

shark	jerung	[dʒɛruŋ]
dolphin	lumba-lumba	[lumba lumbə]
whale	ikan paus	[ikan paus]

crab	ketam	[kɛtam]
jellyfish	ubur-ubur	[ubur ubur]
octopus	sotong kurita	[sotoŋ kuritə]

| starfish | tapak sulaiman | [tapak sulajman] |
| sea urchin | landak laut | [landak laut] |

seahorse	kuda laut	[kuda laut]
oyster	tiram	[tiram]
shrimp	udang	[udaŋ]
lobster	udang karang	[udaŋ karaŋ]
spiny lobster	udang krai	[udaŋ kraj]

92. Amphibians. Reptiles

snake	ular	[ular]
venomous (snake)	beracun	[bɛratʃun]
viper	ular beludak	[ular bɛluda]
cobra	kobra	[kobrə]
python	ular sawa	[ular savə]
boa	ular boa	[ular boə]
grass snake	ular cincin emas	[ular tʃintʃin ɛmas]
rattle snake	ular orok-orok	[ular orok oro]
anaconda	ular anaconda	[ular anakondə]
lizard	cicak	[tʃitʃa]
iguana	iguana	[iguanə]
monitor lizard	biawak	[biavа]
salamander	salamander	[salamandɛr]
chameleon	sumpah-sumpah	[sumpah sumpah]
scorpion	kala jengking	[kala dʒɛŋkiŋ]
turtle	kura-kura	[kura kurə]
frog	katak	[kata]
toad	katak puru	[katak puru]
crocodile	buaya	[buajə]

93. Insects

insect, bug	serangga	[sɛraŋgə]
butterfly	rama-rama	[rama ramə]
ant	semut	[sɛmut]
fly	lalat	[lalat]
mosquito	nyamuk	[njamu]
beetle	kumbang	[kumbaŋ]
wasp	penyengat	[pɛnjeŋat]
bee	lebah	[lɛbah]
bumblebee	kumbang	[kumbaŋ]
gadfly (botfly)	lalat kerbau	[lalat kɛrbau]
spider	labah-labah	[labah labah]
spiderweb	sarang labah-labah	[saraŋ labah labah]

dragonfly	**pepatung**	[pɛpatuŋ]
grasshopper	**belalang**	[bɛlalaŋ]
moth (night butterfly)	**kupu-kupu**	[kupu kupu]
cockroach	**lipas**	[lipas]
tick	**cengkenit**	[ʧɛŋkɛnit]
flea	**pinjal**	[pinʤal]
midge	**agas**	[agas]
locust	**belalang juta**	[bɛlalaŋ ʤutə]
snail	**siput**	[siput]
cricket	**cengkerik**	[ʧɛŋkri]
lightning bug	**kelip-kelip**	[klip klip]
ladybug	**kumbang kura-Kura**	[kumbaŋ kura kurə]
cockchafer	**kumbang kabai**	[kumbaŋ kabaj]
leech	**lintah**	[lintah]
caterpillar	**ulat bulu**	[ulat bulu]
earthworm	**cacing**	[ʧatʃiŋ]
larva	**larva**	[larvə]

FLORA

T&P Books Publishing

tree	**pokok**	[poko]
deciduous (adj)	**daun luruh**	[daun luruh]
coniferous (adj)	**konifer**	[konifer]
evergreen (adj)	**malar hijau**	[malar hiʤau]
apple tree	**pokok epal**	[pokok epal]
pear tree	**pokok pear**	[pokok pɛar]
sweet cherry tree	**pokok ceri manis**	[pokok ʧeri manis]
sour cherry tree	**pokok ceri**	[pokok ʧeri]
plum tree	**pokok plam**	[pokok plam]
birch	**pokok birch**	[pokok 'bøʧ]
oak	**oak**	[ou]
linden tree	**pokok linden**	[pokok linden]
aspen	**pokok aspen**	[pokok aspen]
maple	**pokok mapel**	[pokok mapel]
spruce	**pokok fir**	[pokok fir]
pine	**pokok pain**	[pokok pajn]
larch	**pokok larch**	[pokok larʧ]
fir tree	**fir**	[fir]
cedar	**pokok cedar**	[pokok sidɛr]
poplar	**pokok poplar**	[pokok poplar]
rowan	**pokok rowan**	[pokok rovan]
willow	**pokok willow**	[pokok villou]
alder	**pokok alder**	[pokok alder]
beech	**pokok bic**	[pokok biʧ]
elm	**pokok elm**	[pokok ɛlm]
ash (tree)	**pokok abu**	[pokok abu]
chestnut	**berangan**	[bɛraŋan]
magnolia	**magnolia**	[magnoliə]
palm tree	**palma**	[palmə]
cypress	**pokok cipres**	[pokok ʧipres]
mangrove	**bakau**	[bakau]
baobab	**baobab**	[baobab]
eucalyptus	**eukaliptus**	[ɛukaliptus]
sequoia	**sequoia**	[sekuojə]

95. Shrubs

bush	**pokok**	[poko]
shrub	**pokok renek**	[pokok rene]
grapevine	**pokok anggur**	[pokok aŋgur]
vineyard	**kebun anggur**	[qbun aŋgur]
raspberry bush	**pokok raspberi**	[pokok rasberi]
blackcurrant bush	**pokok beri hitam**	[pokok kismis hitam]
redcurrant bush	**pokok kismis merah**	[pokok kismis merah]
gooseberry bush	**pokok gusberi**	[pokok gusberi]
acacia	**pokok akasia**	[pokok akasiə]
barberry	**pokok barberi**	[pokok barberi]
jasmine	**melati**	[m'lati]
juniper	**pokok juniper**	[pokok dʒuniper]
rosebush	**pokok mawar**	[pokok mavar]
dog rose	**brayer**	[brajer]

96. Fruits. Berries

fruit	**buah**	[buah]
fruits	**buah-buahan**	[buah buahan]
apple	**epal**	[epal]
pear	**buah pear**	[buah pear]
plum	**plam**	[plam]
strawberry (garden ~)	**strawberi**	[stroberi]
sour cherry	**buah ceri**	[buah tʃeri]
sweet cherry	**ceri manis**	[tʃeri manis]
grape	**anggur**	[aŋgur]
raspberry	**raspberi**	[rasberi]
blackcurrant	**beri hitam**	[beri hitam]
redcurrant	**buah kismis merah**	[buah kismis merah]
gooseberry	**buah gusberi**	[buah gusberi]
cranberry	**kranberi**	[kranberi]
orange	**jeruk manis**	[dʒeruk manis]
mandarin	**limau mandarin**	[limau mandarin]
pineapple	**nanas**	[nanas]
banana	**pisang**	[pisaŋ]
date	**buah kurma**	[buah kurmə]
lemon	**lemon**	[lemon]
apricot	**aprikot**	[aprikot]

peach	pic	[piʧ]
kiwi	kiwi	[kivi]
grapefruit	limau gedang	[limau gɛdaŋ]

berry	buah beri	[buah beri]
berries	buah-buah beri	[buah buah beri]
cowberry	cowberry	[kauberi]
wild strawberry	strawberi	[stroberi]
bilberry	buah bilberi	[buah bilberi]

97. Flowers. Plants

| flower | bunga | [buŋə] |
| bouquet (of flowers) | jambak bunga | [dʒambak buŋə] |

rose (flower)	mawar	[mavar]
tulip	tulip	[tulip]
carnation	bunga teluki	[buŋa tɛluki]
gladiolus	bunga gladiola	[buŋa gladiolə]

cornflower	bunga butang	[buŋa butaŋ]
harebell	bunga loceng	[buŋa loʧɛŋ]
dandelion	dandelion	[dandelion]
camomile	bunga camomile	[buŋa kɛmomajl]

aloe	lidah buaya	[lidah buajə]
cactus	kaktus	[kaktus]
rubber plant, ficus	pokok ara	[pokok arə]

lily	bunga lili	[buŋa lili]
geranium	geranium	[geranium]
hyacinth	bunga lembayung	[buŋa lɛmbajuŋ]

mimosa	bunga semalu	[buŋa sɛmalu]
narcissus	bunga narsisus	[buŋa narsisus]
nasturtium	bunga nasturtium	[buŋa nasturtium]

orchid	anggerik, okid	[aŋgrik], [okid]
peony	bunga peony	[buŋa peoni]
violet	bunga violet	[buŋa violet]

pansy	bunga pansy	[buŋa pɛnsi]
forget-me-not	bunga jangan lupakan daku	[buŋa dʒaŋan lupakan daku]
daisy	bunga daisi	[buŋa dajsi]

poppy	bunga popi	[buŋa popi]
hemp	hem	[hem]
mint	mint	[mint]
lily of the valley	lili lembah	[lili lɛmbah]

snowdrop	bunga titisan salji	[buŋa titisan saldʒi]
nettle	netel	[netel]
sorrel	sorrel	[sorel]
water lily	bunga telepok	[buŋa tɛlepo]
fern	paku-pakis	[paku pakis]
lichen	liken	[liken]

conservatory (greenhouse)	rumah hijau	[rumah hidʒau]
lawn	lon	[lon]
flowerbed	batas bunga	[batas buŋə]

plant	tumbuhan	[tumbuhan]
grass	rumput	[rumput]
blade of grass	sehelai rumput	[sɛhelaj rumput]

leaf	daun	[daun]
petal	kelopak	[kɛlopa]
stem	batang	[bataŋ]
tuber	ubi	[ubi]

| young plant (shoot) | tunas | [tunas] |
| thorn | duri | [duri] |

to blossom (vi)	berbunga	[bɛrbuŋə]
to fade, to wither	layu	[laju]
smell (odor)	bau	[bau]
to cut (flowers)	memotong	[mɛmotoŋ]
to pick (a flower)	memetik	[mɛmɛti]

98. Cereals, grains

grain	biji-bijian	[bidʒi bidʒian]
cereal crops	padi-padian	[padi padian]
ear (of barley, etc.)	bulir	[bulir]

wheat	gandum	[gandum]
rye	rai	[raj]
oats	oat	[oat]
millet	sekoi	[sɛkoj]
barley	barli	[barli]

corn	jagung	[dʒaguŋ]
rice	beras	[bras]
buckwheat	bakwit	[bakvit]

pea plant	kacang sepat	[katʃaŋ sɛpat]
kidney bean	kacang buncis	[katʃaŋ buntʃis]
soy	kacang soya	[katʃaŋ sojə]
lentil	kacang lentil	[katʃaŋ lentil]
beans (pulse crops)	kacang	[katʃaŋ]

COUNTRIES OF
THE WORLD

T&P Books Publishing

Afghanistan	**Afghanistan**	[afɣanistan]
Albania	**Albania**	[albaniə]
Argentina	**Argentina**	[argentinə]
Armenia	**Armenia**	[armeniə]
Australia	**Australia**	[australiə]
Austria	**Austria**	[ostriə]
Azerbaijan	**Azerbaijan**	[azerbajdʒan]
The Bahamas	**Kepulauan Bahamas**	[kɛpulawan bahamas]
Bangladesh	**Bangladesh**	[baŋladeʃ]
Belarus	**Belarus**	[belarus]
Belgium	**Belgium**	[beldʒem]
Bolivia	**Bolivia**	[boliviə]
Bosnia and Herzegovina	**Bosnia-Herzegovina**	[bosnia hɛttsigovinə]
Brazil	**Brazil**	[brazil]
Bulgaria	**Bulgaria**	[bulgariə]
Cambodia	**Kemboja**	[kembodʒə]
Canada	**Kanada**	[kanadə]
Chile	**Chile**	[tʃili]
China	**China**	[tʃinə]
Colombia	**Colombia**	[kolombiə]
Croatia	**Croatia**	[krouɛjʃə]
Cuba	**Cuba**	[kjubə]
Cyprus	**Cyprus**	[sajprɛs]
Czech Republic	**Republik Czech**	[republik tʃeh]
Denmark	**Denmark**	[denmar]
Dominican Republic	**Republik Dominika**	[republik dominikə]
Ecuador	**Ecuador**	[ɛkuador]
Egypt	**Mesir**	[mɛsir]
England	**Inggeris**	[iŋgris]
Estonia	**Estonia**	[estoniə]
Finland	**Finland**	[finlɛnd]
France	**Perancis**	[prantʃis]
French Polynesia	**Polinesia Perancis**	[polinesia prantʃis]
Georgia	**Georgia**	[dʒodʒiə]
Germany	**Jerman**	[dʒerman]
Ghana	**Ghana**	[ɣanə]
Great Britain	**Great Britain**	[grejt britɛn]
Greece	**Greece**	[gris]
Haiti	**Haiti**	[hejiti]
Hungary	**Hungary**	[haŋɛri]

100.   Countries. Part 2

Iceland	Iceland	[ajslɛnd]
India	India	[indiǝ]
Indonesia	Indonesia	[indonesiǝ]
Iran	Iran	[iran]
Iraq	Iraq	[irak]
Ireland	Ireland	[ajɛlɛnd]
Israel	Israel	[izrael]
Italy	Itali	[itali]
Jamaica	Jamaica	[dʒamajkǝ]
Japan	Jepun	[dʒepun]
Jordan	Jordan	[dʒodɛn]
Kazakhstan	Kazakhstan	[kazahstan]
Kenya	Kenya	[keniǝ]
Kirghizia	Kirgizia	[kirgiziǝ]
Kuwait	Kuwait	[kuvejt]
Laos	Laos	[laos]
Latvia	Latvia	[latviǝ]
Lebanon	Lubnan	[lubnan]
Libya	Libya	[libiǝ]
Liechtenstein	Liechtenstein	[lihtenstajn]
Lithuania	Lithuania	[lituaniǝ]
Luxembourg	Luxembourg	[laksemburg]
Macedonia (Republic of ~)	Macedonia	[masedoniǝ]
Madagascar	Madagascar	[madagaskar]
Malaysia	Malaysia	[malajsiǝ]
Malta	Malta	[maltǝ]
Mexico	Mexico	[meksiko]
Moldova, Moldavia	Moldavia	[moldavijǝ]
Monaco	Monaco	[monekou]
Mongolia	Mongolia	[moŋoliǝ]
Montenegro	Montenegro	[montenegro]
Morocco	Maghribi	[maɣribi]
Myanmar	Myanmar	[mjanmar]
Namibia	Namibia	[namibiǝ]
Nepal	Nepal	[nepal]
Netherlands	Belanda	[blandǝ]
New Zealand	New Zealand	[nju zilɛnd]
North Korea	Korea Utara	[korea utarǝ]
Norway	Norway	[norvej]

101.   Countries. Part 3

| Pakistan | Pakistan | [pakistan] |
| Palestine | Palestine | [palestin] |

Panama	Panama	[panamə]
Paraguay	Paraguay	[paraguaj]
Peru	Peru	[peru]
Poland	Poland	[polɛnd]
Portugal	Portugal	[portugal]
Romania	Romania	[romaniə]
Russia	Rusia	[rusiə]

Saudi Arabia	Saudi Arabia	[saudi arabiə]
Scotland	Scotland	[skotlɛnd]
Senegal	Senegal	[senegal]
Serbia	Serbia	[serbiə]
Slovakia	Slovakia	[slovakiə]
Slovenia	Slovenia	[sloveniə]

South Africa	Afrika Selatan	[afrika sɛlatan]
South Korea	Korea Selatan	[korea sɛlatan]
Spain	Sepanyol	[spanjol]
Suriname	Suriname	[surinam]
Sweden	Sweden	[svidɛn]
Switzerland	Switzerland	[svizelɛnd]
Syria	Syria	[siriə]

Taiwan	Taiwan	[tajvan]
Tajikistan	Tajikistan	[tadʒikistan]
Tanzania	Tanzania	[tanzaniə]
Tasmania	Tasmania	[tasmaniə]
Thailand	Thailand	[tailand]
Tunisia	Tunisia	[tunisiə]
Turkey	Turki	[turki]
Turkmenistan	Turkmenistan	[turkmenistan]

Ukraine	Ukraine	[jukrejn]
United Arab Emirates	Emiriah Arab Bersatu	[ɛmiria arab bɛrsatu]
United States of America	Amerika Syarikat	[amerika çarikat]
Uruguay	Uruguay	[uruguaj]
Uzbekistan	Uzbekistan	[uzbekistan]

Vatican	Vatican	[vɛtiken]
Venezuela	Venezuela	[venezuelə]
Vietnam	Vietnam	[vjetnam]
Zanzibar	Zanzibar	[zanzibar]

GASTRONOMIC GLOSSARY

This section contains a lot of
words and terms associated
with food. This dictionary will
make it easier for you to
understand the menu at a
restaurant and choose
the right dish

T&P Books Publishing

English-Malay gastronomic glossary

aftertaste	**rasa kesan**	[rasa kɛsan]
almond	**badam**	[badam]
anise	**lawang**	[lavaŋ]
aperitif	**aperitif**	[aperitif]
appetite	**selera**	[sɛlerə]
appetizer	**pembuka selera**	[pɛmbuka sɛlerə]
apple	**epal**	[epal]
apricot	**aprikot**	[aprikot]
artichoke	**articok**	[artitʃo]
asparagus	**asparagus**	[asparagus]
Atlantic salmon	**salmon Atlantik**	[salmon atlanti]
avocado	**avokado**	[avokado]
bacon	**dendeng babi**	[deŋdeŋ babi]
banana	**pisang**	[pisaŋ]
barley	**barli**	[barli]
bartender	**pelayan bar**	[pɛlajan bar]
basil	**kemangi**	[kɛmaŋi]
bay leaf	**daun bay**	[daun bej]
beans	**kacang**	[katʃaŋ]
beef	**daging lembu**	[dagiŋ lɛmbu]
beer	**bir**	[bir]
beet	**rut bit**	[rut bit]
bell pepper	**lada**	[ladə]
berries	**buah-buah beri**	[buah buah beri]
berry	**buah beri**	[buah beri]
bilberry	**buah bilberi**	[buah bilberi]
birch bolete	**cendawan boletus birc**	[tʃɛndavan boletus birtʃ]
bitter	**pahit**	[pahit]
black coffee	**kopi O**	[kopi o]
black pepper	**lada hitam**	[lada hitam]
black tea	**teh hitam**	[te hitam]
blackberry	**beri hitam**	[beri hitam]
blackcurrant	**buah kismis hitam**	[buah kismis hitam]
boiled	**rebus**	[rɛbus]
bottle opener	**pembuka botol**	[pɛmbuka botol]
bread	**roti**	[roti]
breakfast	**makan pagi**	[makan pagi]
bream	**ikan bream**	[ikan brim]
broccoli	**broccoli**	[brokoli]
Brussels sprouts	**kubis Brussels**	[kubis brasels]
buckwheat	**bakwit**	[bakvit]
butter	**mentega**	[mɛntegə]
buttercream	**krim**	[krim]
cabbage	**kubis**	[kubis]

cake	kuih	[kuih]
cake	kek	[ke]
calorie	kalori	[kalori]
can opener	pembuka tin	[pɛmbuka tin]
candy	gula-gula	[gula gulə]
canned food	makanan dalam tin	[makanan dalam tin]
cappuccino	cappuccino	[kaputʃino]
caraway	jintan putih	[dʒintan putih]
carbohydrates	karbohidrat	[karbohidrat]
carbonated	bergas	[bɛrgas]
carp	ikan kap	[ikan kap]
carrot	lobak merah	[lobak merah]
catfish	ikan keli	[ikan kli]
cauliflower	bunga kubis	[buŋa kubis]
caviar	caviar	[kaviar]
celery	saderi	[sadɛri]
cep	boletus	[boletus]
cereal crops	padi-padian	[padi padian]
champagne	champagne	[ʃampejn]
chanterelle	cendawan chanterelle	[tʃɛndavan tʃɛnterel]
check	bil	[bil]
cheese	keju	[kɛdʒu]
chewing gum	gula-gula getah	[gula gula gɛtah]
chicken	ayam	[ajam]
chocolate	coklat	[tʃoklat]
chocolate	coklat	[tʃoklat]
cinnamon	kayu manis	[kaju manis]
clear soup	sup kosong	[sup kosoŋ]
cloves	cengkeh	[tʃeŋkeh]
cocktail	koktel	[koktel]
coconut	buah kelapa	[buah klapə]
cod	ikan kod	[ikan kod]
coffee	kopi	[kopi]
coffee with milk	kopi susu	[kopi susu]
cognac	cognac	[konjak]
cold	sejuk	[sɛdʒu]
condensed milk	susu pekat	[susu pɛkat]
condiment	perasa	[pɛrasə]
confectionery	kuih-muih	[kuih muih]
cookies	biskit	[biskit]
coriander	ketumbar	[kɛtumbar]
corkscrew	skru gabus	[skru gabus]
corn	jagung	[dʒaguŋ]
corn	jagung	[dʒaguŋ]
cornflakes	emping jagung	[ɛmpiŋ dʒaguŋ]
course, dish	hidangan	[hidaŋan]
cowberry	cowberry	[kauberi]
crab	ketam	[kɛtam]
cranberry	kranberi	[kranberi]
cream	krim	[krim]
crumb	remah	[remah]
crustaceans	krustasia	[krustasiə]

cucumber	**timun**	[timun]
cuisine	**masakan**	[masakan]
cup	**cawan**	[ʧavan]
dark beer	**bir hitam**	[bir hitam]
date	**buah kurma**	[buah kurmə]
death cap	**cendavan kep kematian**	[ʧɛndavan kep kɛmatian]
dessert	**pencuci mulut**	[pɛnʧuʧi mulut]
diet	**diet**	[diet]
dill	**jintan hitam**	[ʤintan hitam]
dinner	**makan malam**	[makan malam]
dried	**dikeringkan**	[dikɛriŋkan]
drinking water	**air minum**	[air minum]
duck	**itik**	[iti]
ear	**bulir**	[bulir]
edible mushroom	**cendawan yang boleh dimakan**	[ʧɛndavan jaŋ bole dimakan]
eel	**ikan keli**	[ikan kli]
egg	**telur**	[tɛlur]
egg white	**putih telur**	[putih tɛlur]
egg yolk	**kuning telur**	[kuniŋ tɛlur]
eggplant	**terung**	[tɛruŋ]
eggs	**telur-telur**	[tɛlur tɛlur]
Enjoy your meal!	**Selamat jamu selera!**	[sɛlamat ʤamu sɛlerə]
fats	**lemak**	[lɛma]
fig	**buah tin**	[buah tin]
filling	**inti**	[inti]
fish	**ikan**	[ikan]
flatfish	**ikan sebelah**	[ikan sɛblah]
flour	**tepung**	[tɛpuŋ]
fly agaric	**cendawan Amanita muscaria**	[ʧɛndavan amanita muskariə]
food	**makanan**	[makanan]
fork	**garpu**	[garpu]
freshly squeezed juice	**jus segar**	[ʤus sɛgar]
fried	**goreng**	[goreŋ]
fried eggs	**telur mata kerbau**	[tɛlur mata kerbau]
frozen	**sejuk beku**	[sɛʤuk bɛku]
fruit	**buah**	[buah]
fruits	**buah-buahan**	[buah buahan]
game	**burung buruan**	[buruŋ buruan]
gammon	**gamon**	[gamon]
garlic	**bawang putih**	[bavaŋ putih]
gin	**gin**	[ʤin]
ginger	**halia**	[haliə]
glass	**gelas**	[glas]
glass	**gelas**	[glas]
goose	**angsa**	[aŋsə]
gooseberry	**buah gusberi**	[buah gusberi]
grain	**biji-bijian**	[biʤi biʤian]
grape	**anggur**	[aŋgur]
grapefruit	**limau gedang**	[limau gɛdaŋ]
green tea	**teh hijau**	[te hiʤau]

greens	ulam-ulaman	[ulam ulaman]
groats	bijirin berkupas	[bidʒirin bɛrkupas]
halibut	ikan halibut	[ikan halibut]
ham	ham	[ham]
hamburger	bahan kisar	[bahan kisar]
hamburger	hamburger	[hamburger]
hazelnut	kacang hazel	[katʃaŋ hazel]
herring	ikan hering	[ikan hɛriŋ]
honey	madu	[madu]
horseradish	remunggai	[rɛmuŋgaj]
hot	panas	[panas]
ice	ais	[ajs]
ice-cream	ais krim	[ajs krim]
instant coffee	kopi segera	[kopi sɛgɛrə]
jam	jem	[dʒɛm]
jam	jem buah-buahan utuh	[dʒem buah buahan utuh]
juice	jus	[dʒus]
kidney bean	kacang buncis	[katʃaŋ buntʃis]
kiwi	kiwi	[kivi]
knife	pisau	[pisau]
lamb	daging bebiri	[dagiŋ bɛbiri]
lemon	lemon	[lemon]
lemonade	limonad	[limonad]
lentil	kacang lentil	[katʃaŋ lentil]
lettuce	pokok salad	[pokok salad]
light beer	bir putih	[bir putih]
liqueur	likur	[likur]
liquors	arak	[ara]
liver	hati	[hati]
lunch	makan tengah hari	[makan tɛŋah hari]
mackerel	ikan tenggiri	[ikan tɛŋgiri]
mandarin	limau mandarin	[limau mandarin]
mango	mempelam	[mɛmpɛlam]
margarine	marjerin	[mardʒɛrin]
marmalade	marmalad	[marmalad]
mashed potatoes	kentang lecek	[kɛntaŋ letʃe]
mayonnaise	mayonis	[majonis]
meat	daging	[dagiŋ]
melon	tembikai susu	[tembikaj susu]
menu	menu	[menu]
milk	susu	[susu]
milkshake	susu kocak	[susu kotʃa]
millet	sekoi	[sɛkoj]
mineral water	air galian	[air galian]
morel	cendawan morel	[tʃɛndavan morel]
mushroom	cendawan	[tʃɛndavan]
mustard	sawi	[savi]
non-alcoholic	tanpa alkohol	[tanpa alkohol]
noodles	mie	[mi]
oats	oat	[oat]
olive oil	minyak zaitun	[minjak zaɪtun]
olives	buah zaitun	[buah zajtun]

omelet	**telur dadar**	[tɛlur dadar]
onion	**bawang**	[bavaŋ]
orange	**jeruk manis**	[dʒeruk manis]
orange juice	**jus jeruk manis**	[dʒus dʒɛruk manis]
orange-cap boletus	**cendawan topi jingga**	[tʃɛndavan topi dʒiŋgə]
oyster	**tiram**	[tiram]
pâté	**pate**	[patɛ]
papaya	**betik**	[bɛti]
paprika	**paprik**	[papri]
parsley	**parsli**	[parsli]
pasta	**pasta**	[pastə]
pea	**kacang sepat**	[katʃaŋ sɛpat]
peach	**pic**	[pitʃ]
peanut	**kacang tanah**	[katʃaŋ tanah]
pear	**buah pear**	[buah pear]
peel	**kulit**	[kulit]
perch	**ikan puyu**	[ikan puju]
pickled	**dijeruk**	[didʒɛru]
pie	**pai**	[paj]
piece	**potongan**	[potoŋan]
pike	**ikan paik**	[ikan paj]
pike perch	**ikan zander**	[ikan zander]
pineapple	**nanas**	[nanas]
pistachios	**pistasio**	[pistasio]
pizza	**piza**	[pizə]
plate	**pinggan**	[piŋgan]
plum	**plum**	[plam]
poisonous mushroom	**cendawan yang beracun**	[tʃɛndavan jaŋ bɛratʃun]
pomegranate	**buah delima**	[buah dɛlimə]
pork	**daging babi**	[dagiŋ babi]
porridge	**bubur**	[bubur]
portion	**hidangan**	[hidaŋan]
potato	**kentang**	[kɛntaŋ]
proteins	**protein**	[protein]
pub, bar	**bar**	[bar]
pudding	**puding**	[pudiŋ]
pumpkin	**labu**	[labu]
rabbit	**arnab**	[arnab]
radish	**lobak**	[loba]
raisin	**kismis**	[kismis]
raspberry	**raspberi**	[rasberi]
recipe	**resipi**	[rɛsipi]
red pepper	**lada merah**	[lada merah]
red wine	**wain merah**	[vajn merah]
redcurrant	**buah kismis merah**	[buah kismis merah]
refreshing drink	**minuman segar**	[minuman sɛgar]
rice	**beras, nasi**	[bras], [nasi]
rum	**rum**	[ram]
russula	**cendawan rusula**	[tʃɛndavan rusulə]
rye	**rai**	[raj]
saffron	**safron**	[safron]
salad	**salad**	[salad]

salmon	salmon	[salmon]
salt	garam	[garam]
salty	masin	[masin]
sandwich	sandwic	[sandvitʃ]
sardine	sadin	[sadin]
sauce	saus	[saus]
saucer	alas cawan	[alas tʃavan]
sausage	sosej worst	[sosedʒ vorst]
seafood	makanan laut	[makanan laut]
sesame	bijan	[bidʒan]
shark	jerung	[dʒɛruŋ]
shrimp	udang	[udaŋ]
side dish	garnish	[garniʃ]
slice	irisan	[irisan]
smoked	salai	[salaj]
soft drink	minuman ringan	[minuman riŋan]
soup	sup	[sup]
soup spoon	sudu makan	[sudu makan]
sour cherry	buah ceri	[buah tʃeri]
sour cream	krim asam	[krim asam]
soy	kacang soya	[katʃaŋ sojə]
spaghetti	spaghetti	[spaɣeti]
sparkling	bergas	[bɛrgas]
spice	rempah-rempah	[rempah rempah]
spinach	bayam	[bajam]
spiny lobster	udang krai	[udaŋ kraj]
spoon	sudu	[sudu]
squid	cumi-cumi	[tʃumi tʃumi]
steak	stik	[sti]
still	tanpa gas	[tanpa gas]
strawberry	strawberi	[stroberi]
sturgeon	ikan sturgeon	[ikan sturgeon]
sugar	gula	[gulə]
sunflower oil	minyak bunga matahari	[minjak buŋa matahari]
sweet	manis	[manis]
sweet cherry	ceri manis	[tʃeri manis]
taste, flavor	rasa	[rasə]
tasty	sedap	[sɛdap]
tea	teh	[te]
teaspoon	sudu teh	[sudu teh]
tip	tip	[tip]
tomato	tomato	[tomato]
tomato juice	jus tomato	[dʒus tomato]
tongue	lidah	[lidah]
toothpick	cungkil gigi	[tʃuŋkil gigi]
trout	ikan trout	[ikan trout]
tuna	tuna	[tunə]
turkey	ayam belanda	[ajam blandə]
turnip	turnip	[turnip]
veal	daging anak lembu	[dagiŋ anak lembu]
vegetable oil	minyak sayur	[minjak sajur]
vegetables	sayuran	[sajuran]

vegetarian	vegetarian	[vegetarian]
vegetarian	vegetarian	[vegetarian]
vermouth	vermouth	[vermut]
vienna sausage	sosej	[sosedʒ]
vinegar	cuka	[ʧukə]
vitamin	vitamin	[vitamin]
vodka	vodka	[vodkə]
wafers	wafer	[vafɛr]
waiter	pelayan	[pɛlajan]
waitress	pelayan perempuan	[pɛlajan pɛrɛmpuan]
walnut	walnut	[volnat]
water	air	[air]
watermelon	tembikai	[tembikaj]
wheat	gandum	[gandum]
whiskey	wiski	[viski]
white wine	wain putih	[vajn putih]
wild strawberry	strawberi	[stroberi]
wine	wain	[vajn]
wine list	kad wain	[kad vajn]
with ice	dengan ais	[dɛŋan ajs]
yogurt	yogurt	[jogurt]
zucchini	labu kuning	[labu kuniŋ]

Malay-English gastronomic glossary

air	[air]	water
air galian	[air galian]	mineral water
air minum	[air minum]	drinking water
ais	[ajs]	ice
ais krim	[ajs krim]	ice-cream
alas cawan	[alas ʧavan]	saucer
anggur	[aŋgur]	grape
angsa	[aŋsə]	goose
aperitif	[aperitif]	aperitif
aprikot	[aprikot]	apricot
arak	[ara]	liquors
arnab	[arnab]	rabbit
articok	[artiʧo]	artichoke
asparagus	[asparagus]	asparagus
avokado	[avokado]	avocado
ayam	[ajam]	chicken
ayam belanda	[ajam blandə]	turkey
badam	[badam]	almond
bahan kisar	[bahan kisar]	hamburger
bakwit	[bakvit]	buckwheat
bar	[bar]	pub, bar
barli	[barli]	barley
bawang	[bavaŋ]	onion
bawang putih	[bavaŋ putih]	garlic
bayam	[bajam]	spinach
beras, nasi	[bras], [nasi]	rice
bergas	[bɛrgas]	carbonated
bergas	[bɛrgas]	sparkling
beri hitam	[beri hitam]	blackberry
betik	[bɛti]	papaya
bijan	[bidʒan]	sesame
biji-bijian	[bidʒi bidʒian]	grain
bijirin berkupas	[bidʒirin bɛrkupas]	groats
bil	[bil]	check
bir	[bir]	beer
bir hitam	[bir hitam]	dark beer
bir putih	[bir putih]	light beer
biskit	[biskit]	cookies
boletus	[boletus]	cep
broccoli	[brokoli]	broccoli
buah	[buah]	fruit
buah beri	[buah beri]	berry
buah bilberi	[buah bilberi]	bilberry
buah ceri	[buah ʧeri]	sour cherry

buah delima	[buah dɛlimə]	pomegranate
buah gusberi	[buah gusberi]	gooseberry
buah kelapa	[buah klapə]	coconut
buah kismis hitam	[buah kismis hitam]	blackcurrant
buah kismis merah	[buah kismis merah]	redcurrant
buah kurma	[buah kurmə]	date
buah pear	[buah pear]	pear
buah tin	[buah tin]	fig
buah zaitun	[buah zajtun]	olives
buah-buah beri	[buah buah beri]	berries
buah-buahan	[buah buahan]	fruits
bubur	[bubur]	porridge
bulir	[bulir]	ear
bunga kubis	[buɲa kubis]	cauliflower
burung buruan	[buruŋ buruan]	game
cappuccino	[kaputʃino]	cappuccino
caviar	[kaviar]	caviar
cawan	[tʃavan]	cup
cendawan	[tʃɛndavan]	mushroom
cendawan Amanita muscaria	[tʃɛndavan amanita muskariə]	fly agaric
cendawan boletus birc	[tʃɛndavan boletus birtʃ]	birch bolete
cendawan chanterelle	[tʃɛndavan tʃɛnterel]	chanterelle
cendawan kep kematian	[tʃɛndavan kep kɛmatian]	death cap
cendawan morel	[tʃɛndavan morel]	morel
cendawan rusula	[tʃɛndavan rusulə]	russula
cendawan topi jingga	[tʃɛndavan topi dʒiŋgə]	orange-cap boletus
cendawan yang beracun	[tʃɛndavan jaŋ bɛratʃun]	poisonous mushroom
cendawan yang boleh dimakan	[tʃɛndavan jaŋ bole dimakan]	edible mushroom
cengkeh	[tʃeŋkeh]	cloves
ceri manis	[tʃeri manis]	sweet cherry
champagne	[ʃampejn]	champagne
cognac	[konjak]	cognac
coklat	[tʃoklat]	chocolate
coklat	[tʃoklat]	chocolate
cowberry	[kauberi]	cowberry
cuka	[tʃukə]	vinegar
cumi-cumi	[tʃumi tʃumi]	squid
cungkil gigi	[tʃuŋkil gigi]	toothpick
daging	[dagiŋ]	meat
daging anak lembu	[dagiŋ anak lembu]	veal
daging babi	[dagiŋ babi]	pork
daging bebiri	[dagiŋ bɛbiri]	lamb
daging lembu	[dagiŋ lɛmbu]	beef
daun bay	[daun bej]	bay leaf
dendeng babi	[deŋdeŋ babi]	bacon
dengan ais	[dɛŋan ajs]	with ice
diet	[diet]	diet
dijeruk	[didʒɛru]	pickled
dikeringkan	[dikɛriŋkan]	dried
emping jagung	[ɛmpiŋ dʒaguŋ]	cornflakes

epal	[epal]	apple
gamon	[gamon]	gammon
gandum	[gandum]	wheat
garam	[garam]	salt
garnish	[garniʃ]	side dish
garpu	[garpu]	fork
gelas	[glas]	glass
gelas	[glas]	glass
gin	[dʒin]	gin
goreng	[goreŋ]	fried
gula	[gulə]	sugar
gula-gula	[gula gulə]	candy
gula-gula getah	[gula gula gɛtah]	chewing gum
halia	[haliə]	ginger
ham	[ham]	ham
hamburger	[hamburger]	hamburger
hati	[hati]	liver
hidangan	[hidaŋan]	course, dish
hidangan	[hidaŋan]	portion
ikan	[ikan]	fish
ikan bream	[ikan brim]	bream
ikan halibut	[ikan halibut]	halibut
ikan hering	[ikan hɛriŋ]	herring
ikan kap	[ikan kap]	carp
ikan keli	[ikan kli]	eel
ikan keli	[ikan kli]	catfish
ikan kod	[ikan kod]	cod
ikan paik	[ikan paj]	pike
ikan puyu	[ikan puju]	perch
ikan sebelah	[ikan sɛblah]	flatfish
ikan sturgeon	[ikan sturgeon]	sturgeon
ikan tenggiri	[ikan tɛŋiri]	mackerel
ikan trout	[ikan trout]	trout
ikan zander	[ikan zander]	pike perch
inti	[inti]	filling
irisan	[irisan]	slice
itik	[iti]	duck
jagung	[dʒaguŋ]	corn
jagung	[dʒaguŋ]	corn
jem	[dʒɛm]	jam
jem buah-buahan utuh	[dʒem buah buahan utuh]	jam
jeruk manis	[dʒeruk manis]	orange
jerung	[dʒɛruŋ]	shark
jintan hitam	[dʒintan hitam]	dill
jintan putih	[dʒintan putih]	caraway
jus	[dʒus]	juice
jus jeruk manis	[dʒus dʒɛruk manis]	orange juice
jus segar	[dʒus sɛgar]	freshly squeezed juice
jus tomato	[dʒus tomato]	tomato juice
kacang	[katʃaŋ]	beans
kacang buncis	[katʃaŋ buntʃis]	kidney bean
kacang hazel	[katʃaŋ hazel]	hazelnut

kacang lentil	[katʃaŋ lentil]	lentil
kacang sepat	[katʃaŋ sɛpat]	pea
kacang soya	[katʃaŋ sojə]	soy
kacang tanah	[katʃaŋ tanah]	peanut
kad wain	[kad vajn]	wine list
kalori	[kalori]	calorie
karbohidrat	[karbohidrat]	carbohydrates
kayu manis	[kaju manis]	cinnamon
keju	[kɛdʒu]	cheese
kek	[ke]	cake
kemangi	[kɛmaŋi]	basil
kentang	[kɛntaŋ]	potato
kentang lecek	[kɛntaŋ letʃe]	mashed potatoes
ketam	[kɛtam]	crab
ketumbar	[kɛtumbar]	coriander
kismis	[kismis]	raisin
kiwi	[kivi]	kiwi
koktel	[koktel]	cocktail
kopi	[kopi]	coffee
kopi O	[kopi o]	black coffee
kopi segera	[kopi sɛgɛrə]	instant coffee
kopi susu	[kopi susu]	coffee with milk
kranberi	[kranberi]	cranberry
krim	[krim]	cream
krim	[krim]	buttercream
krim asam	[krim asam]	sour cream
krustasia	[krustasiə]	crustaceans
kubis	[kubis]	cabbage
kubis Brussels	[kubis brasels]	Brussels sprouts
kuih	[kuih]	cake
kuih-muih	[kuih muih]	confectionery
kulit	[kulit]	peel
kuning telur	[kuniŋ tɛlur]	egg yolk
labu	[labu]	pumpkin
labu kuning	[labu kuniŋ]	zucchini
lada	[ladə]	bell pepper
lada hitam	[lada hitam]	black pepper
lada merah	[lada merah]	red pepper
lawang	[lavaŋ]	anise
lemak	[lɛma]	fats
lemon	[lemon]	lemon
lidah	[lidah]	tongue
likur	[likur]	liqueur
limau gedang	[limau gɛdaŋ]	grapefruit
limau mandarin	[limau mandarin]	mandarin
limonad	[limonad]	lemonade
lobak	[loba]	radish
lobak merah	[lobak merah]	carrot
madu	[madu]	honey
makan malam	[makan malam]	dinner
makan pagi	[makan pagi]	breakfast
makan tengah hari	[makan tɛŋah hari]	lunch

makanan	[makanan]	food
makanan dalam tin	[makanan dalam tin]	canned food
makanan laut	[makanan laut]	seafood
manis	[manis]	sweet
marjerin	[mardʒɛrin]	margarine
marmalad	[marmalad]	marmalade
masakan	[masakan]	cuisine
masin	[masin]	salty
mayonis	[majonis]	mayonnaise
mempelam	[mɛmpɛlam]	mango
mentega	[mɛntegə]	butter
menu	[menu]	menu
mie	[mi]	noodles
minuman ringan	[minuman riŋan]	soft drink
minuman segar	[minuman sɛgar]	refreshing drink
minyak bunga matahari	[minjak buŋa matahari]	sunflower oil
minyak sayur	[minjak sajur]	vegetable oil
minyak zaitun	[minjak zaɪtun]	olive oil
nanas	[nanas]	pineapple
oat	[oat]	oats
padi-padian	[padi padian]	cereal crops
pahit	[pahit]	bitter
pai	[paj]	pie
panas	[panas]	hot
paprik	[papri]	paprika
parsli	[parsli]	parsley
pasta	[pastə]	pasta
pate	[patɛ]	pâté
pelayan	[pɛlajan]	waiter
pelayan bar	[pɛlajan bar]	bartender
pelayan perempuan	[pɛlajan pɛrɛmpuan]	waitress
pembuka botol	[pɛmbuka botol]	bottle opener
pembuka selera	[pɛmbuka sɛlerə]	appetizer
pembuka tin	[pɛmbuka tin]	can opener
pencuci mulut	[pɛntʃutʃi mulut]	dessert
perasa	[pɛrasə]	condiment
pic	[pitʃ]	peach
pinggan	[piŋgan]	plate
pisang	[pisaŋ]	banana
pisau	[pisau]	knife
pistasio	[pistasio]	pistachios
piza	[pizə]	pizza
plum	[plam]	plum
pokok salad	[pokok salad]	lettuce
potongan	[potoŋan]	piece
protein	[protein]	proteins
puding	[pudiŋ]	pudding
putih telur	[putih tɛlur]	egg white
rai	[raj]	rye
rasa	[rasə]	taste, flavor
rasa kesan	[rasa kɛsan]	aftertaste
raspberi	[rasberi]	raspberry

rebus	[rɛbus]	boiled
remah	[remah]	crumb
rempah-rempah	[rempah rempah]	spice
remunggai	[rɛmuŋgaj]	horseradish
resipi	[rɛsipi]	recipe
roti	[roti]	bread
rum	[ram]	rum
rut bit	[rut bit]	beet
saderi	[sadɛri]	celery
sadin	[sadin]	sardine
safron	[safron]	saffron
salad	[salad]	salad
salai	[salaj]	smoked
salmon	[salmon]	salmon
salmon Atlantik	[salmon atlanti]	Atlantic salmon
sandwic	[sandviʧ]	sandwich
saus	[saus]	sauce
sawi	[savi]	mustard
sayuran	[sajuran]	vegetables
sedap	[sɛdap]	tasty
sejuk	[sɛdʒu]	cold
sejuk beku	[sɛdʒuk bɛku]	frozen
sekoi	[sɛkoj]	millet
Selamat jamu selera!	[sɛlamat dʒamu sɛlerə]	Enjoy your meal!
selera	[sɛlerə]	appetite
skru gabus	[skru gabus]	corkscrew
sosej	[sosedʒ]	vienna sausage
sosej worst	[sosedʒ vorst]	sausage
spaghetti	[spaɣeti]	spaghetti
stik	[sti]	steak
strawberi	[stroberi]	strawberry
strawberi	[stroberi]	wild strawberry
sudu	[sudu]	spoon
sudu makan	[sudu makan]	soup spoon
sudu teh	[sudu teh]	teaspoon
sup	[sup]	soup
sup kosong	[sup kosoŋ]	clear soup
susu	[susu]	milk
susu kocak	[susu koʧa]	milkshake
susu pekat	[susu pɛkat]	condensed milk
tanpa alkohol	[tanpa alkohol]	non-alcoholic
tanpa gas	[tanpa gas]	still
teh	[te]	tea
teh hijau	[te hidʒau]	green tea
teh hitam	[te hitam]	black tea
telur	[tɛlur]	egg
telur dadar	[tɛlur dadar]	omelet
telur mata kerbau	[tɛlur mata kerbau]	fried eggs
telur-telur	[tɛlur tɛlur]	eggs
tembikai	[tembikaj]	watermelon
tembikai susu	[tembikaj susu]	melon
tepung	[tɛpuŋ]	flour

terung	[tɛruŋ]	eggplant
timun	[timun]	cucumber
tip	[tip]	tip
tiram	[tiram]	oyster
tomato	[tomato]	tomato
tuna	[tunə]	tuna
turnip	[turnip]	turnip
udang	[udaŋ]	shrimp
udang krai	[udaŋ kraj]	spiny lobster
ulam-ulaman	[ulam ulaman]	greens
vegetarian	[vegetarian]	vegetarian
vegetarian	[vegetarian]	vegetarian
vermouth	[vermut]	vermouth
vitamin	[vitamin]	vitamin
vodka	[vodkə]	vodka
wafer	[vafɛr]	wafers
wain	[vajn]	wine
wain merah	[vajn merah]	red wine
wain putih	[vajn putih]	white wine
walnut	[volnat]	walnut
wiski	[viski]	whiskey
yogurt	[jogurt]	yogurt

Manufactured by Amazon.ca
Bolton, ON

20909915R00116